Words Fail Us

ALSO BY BOB BLACKBURN

Canadian Cryptic Crosswords (1990)

WORDS FAIL US

Good English and Other Lost Causes

Bob Blackburn

M&S

Canadian Cataloguing in Publication Data

Blackburn, Bob, 1926-
Words fail us: good English and other lost causes

Includes bibliographical references.

ISBN 0-7710-1529-1

1. English language – Errors of usage. I. Title.

PE1460.B53 1993   428.1   C93-093089-4

The publishers acknowledge the support of the Canada Council and the Ontario Arts Council for their publishing program.

The support of the Government of Ontario through the Ministry of Culture and Communications is acknowledged.

Typesetting by M&S, Toronto
Printed and bound in Canada
The paper used in this book is acid free.

McClelland & Stewart Inc.
The Canadian Publishers
481 University Avenue
Toronto, Ontario
M5G 2E9

For Kath

For Clyde, Robin, Liz, and Roxanne

For David, Leanne, Lisa, Michael, Rachel, Robbie, Sara,

Sarah, and Victoria

And for Elsa

Contents

Preface

This is a layman's lament about linguistic anarchy.

I have been supporting my habits for close to a half-century by assembling words for other people to read. I think I have succeeded in informing and occasionally amusing some of those people.

That's about the extent of my qualifications to be writing this book. I wanted to say that up front, lest anyone think I am trying to pass myself off as anything grander than someone who has done well enough as a keyboard drudge.

On a sweltering Toronto day in 1980, I was quaffing beer with a friend and colleague, Douglas Marshall, who was then editor of the monthly magazine *Books in Canada*. We were discussing, as we often did, the declining quality of English usage in newspapers, magazines, and broadcasting (and, I suppose, everywhere else).

He asked me if I would have a shot at writing a regular column on this subject for his magazine. I thought about it, and later told him that I liked the idea but did not feel qualified to take it on. I suggested his purpose would be better served by someone with academic qualifications. He said he would prefer someone who simply wrote for a living and cared about the craft.

I felt diffident about undertaking the column, and I feel diffident about writing this book, but in both cases I felt also that it might be worth doing.

So, in October of 1980, there appeared in *Books in Canada* a column bearing the title "english, our english". It found favour, and continued until the spring of 1988. It might not have changed the world much, but it made a significant contribution to my own education, especially when I was found in error. A discerning readership is a stern teacher.

A common colloquial phrase today is "This is to let you know where I'm coming from". It's ugly, but I'm getting used to it. It serves a purpose, and I think it might be around for a while. I'm going to use it right now. What follows is to let you know where I'm coming from. (Gawd, it *is* ugly.)

I worked for newspapers most of my adult life, mostly as a columnist, sometimes as an editor. I was a staff writer in Ottawa for *The Ottawa Journal* and *The Ottawa Citizen* and in Toronto for *The Toronto Star* and *The Telegram*, in that order. When the last-named paper folded in 1971, I became a freelance writer, but was a daily columnist for *The Toronto Sun* for most of the rest of that decade. I have been a regular or occasional contributor to a few other newspapers and a number of national magazines, and have done an insignificant amount of writing for radio and TV. I was one of the earlier TV columnists in Canada, and kept at it longer than most and longer than I should have or wanted to. I have been a computer enthusiast for about a decade, with a particular interest in computer-based telecommunications, and I have had about 450 cryptic crossword puzzles published (some of which are available in paperback from McClelland & Stewart at a surprisingly affordable price). All these experiences have some effect on what I am writing here.

By mid-century, I had done with formal education and was embarked on a career of writing. I had had a few good teachers, and had been exposed to a few good editors. I didn't know a hell of a lot.

Certainly I didn't know as much as I thought I did, but I did know that I didn't know everything. Now, more than forty years later, I have a much better grasp of the degree of my ignorance. All I can say about it is that I have spent sixty-five years trying with modest zeal to learn the language, and that I have made some progress.

What is in the pages that follow is mostly a collection of errors and undesirable practices that have offended my eye and ear in recent years. It is personal, opinionated, quixotic, and quirky. It might also be called negative. There still is a lot of good writing around, but that's not what this is about. I don't know if there's any point to all this. When I started writing on the subject in *Books in Canada*, Clyde Gilmour, a meticulous writer who was the pre-eminent Canadian film critic for several decades of this century, told me: "I suppose you know you're wasting your time, but by all means carry on." I thought then, and think now, that he was right. I think, also, that more people ought to be digging in their heels and hollering with outrage. There simply isn't enough public discussion on this subject. There are many more qualified than I to do this, but I was, and am, willing to pitch in.

This was the conclusion of my first column in *Books in Canada*:

> Recently I was scanning an article in *Today,* which bills itself "Canada's largest-circulation magazine" (awkward phrase, that), when a most egregious pleonasm leapt from the page to offend my sensibilities. The writer had used the phrase "flaying the hide off someone". As we all know, to flay means to strip off the skin or hide of.
>
> The offending writer was I. The example is cited to make the point that the author of all the above criticism is acutely

aware that he lives in a glass house; however, he has never
minded being stoned.

The closing pun was intended as a warning that I intended to have
some fun from time to time. I did, and I still do, and I heard from
quite a few readers who shared in it. Others occasionally had difficulty spotting the leg-pulls. *Caveat lector.*

There are references in the book to various authorities, some of
which I should list here. *OED* is the *Oxford English Dictionary*, the
first complete edition (1933). *Fowler* is W.H. Fowler, quoted from
his *A Dictionary of Modern English Usage* (second edition, revised
by Sir Ernest Gowers). *RH-II* is *The Random House Dictionary of
the English Language, Second Edition, Unabridged. Bernstein* is
Theodore Bernstein, the author of several books, including *The
Careful Writer. Strunk & White* refers to *The Elements of Style,* by
William Strunk, Jr., and E.B. White. This is one of the handiest little
reference books available, and should be reread (all eighty-five
pages of it) at least once a year. *Quirk* means *A Grammar of Contemporary English* by Randolph Quirk, Sidney Greenbaum, Geoffrey
Leech, and Jan Svartvik. I am not the first one to have found it
simpler to call it just "Quirk". *Webster* is a problem. The name is in
the public domain, and can mean just about anything. In this book,
it will refer to *Webster's New International Dictionary, Second Edition, Unabridged,* published in 1948 by G. & C. Merriam Company
of Springfield, Mass., U.S.A.

CHAPTER 1

Words Fail Us

Words fail us because, as the comic Rodney Dangerfield might say, they don't get no respect.

English is a bitch. Rich, beautiful, capable of rewarding her lovers with undreamt-of delights and rewards, but a bitch, withal. I contend that the way to woo a bitch is certainly not to abuse her. Many disagree with me, and that's why we're in trouble. That's why we keep having to ask each other "You know what I mean?".

Some will regard that paragraph as sexist, but, if you really think about it, it isn't.

This book is mostly about linguistic anarchy. For some four centuries, concerned people have tried mightily to codify rules designed to help English-speaking people understand one another. For the last half-century, unconcerned people have been wantonly frustrating this work. It is not without significance that the same half-century has seen an explosive development in the means of instantaneous mass communications.

The rules aren't great, but they are better than nothing. Now they're going down the drain.

The awful dilemma confronting the careful writer today is the choice between selecting his words according to what they mean or selecting them according to what his audience might think they mean.

We are in a vicious circle. Most of the torrent of writing currently produced for widespread consumption is bad. Most of the people reading it have an inadequate grasp of English because they have not been exposed to good writing.

Words fail us because they are being abused beyond recognition. Dictionaries are no longer of much help. Most of today's lexicographers are of the descriptive school. They believe they have done their work if they have described the current misuse of the language, and feel no obligation to pass judgment on that use.

Generally, today's teachers are victims of the same educational system that now employs them. They did not have good teachers. Today's editors were denied the benefit of working for good editors, and are not qualified to train young writers. Many of today's readers don't understand good writing any better than, or even as well as, they do bad writing.

Much of this book is being written with growing disbelief and despair. I suppose that I am open to being charged with negativism. I try to keep reminding myself that there is still good writing, and there are still people who appreciate it, but the prospects remain bleak. I can think of nothing that has depressed me more than finding, in recent years, an increasing number of errors in *The New Yorker*. There is an enduring legend about its founding editor, Harold Ross. The story has it that an edition was coming out containing the T.S. Eliot quote "Not with a bang but a whimper". Ross was so certain that, somewhere along the line, someone would change *whimper* to *whisper*, that he was found on publication day lying under the presses as they were about to roll, checking the plates to make sure it hadn't happened. Ross is long gone, but for decades his less colourful but no less meticulous successor, William Shawn, went on making any skeptic's search for errors in the end product a mug's game. When Shawn was ousted by a new owner in the 1980s, things started to slide. The sort of standards he and Ross insisted on no longer seemed to matter to the owners. Even at that, I dare say *The New Yorker* is still as carefully edited as any magazine around, but that does not mean as much as it once meant.

School can, should, and still sometimes does give one a lift along the way to literacy, but that's all. Learning to read and write begins at birth (or earlier, some believe). For the most part, people become literate by listening and reading. By the time they get to kindergarten, children should have a considerable vocabulary, and perhaps some rudimentary reading and writing skills.

For the next fifteen years or so, they will get some advice and technical guidance in the classroom. It might not be as good as it was fifty or a hundred years ago, but it should help.

I'm not qualified to talk about our educational system. I haven't kept up with the changing methods of teaching English. It's more than sixty years since I was taught to read, and I don't really remember how it was done, but it was done. It was possible then, and it is possible now, to emerge literate from a provincial school system. This has been demonstrated to me by my children and grandchildren. I don't know, though, that our educational system merits much credit for this. As I recall, it would have been pretty tough in my day for a kid to get through high school without being able to read and write, and obviously this is no longer true. I'm told by teachers in the Ontario system that they are required to promote pupils regardless of inadequate language achievement, and I know that many of today's teachers wouldn't really know the difference, since they are products of the systems they now serve. But the trouble lies at least as much in the home as in the school.

Mostly, the degree of literacy we achieve in a lifetime depends, all else being equal, on what we read and hear. That means we're in trouble.

The greatest share of culpability for that trouble lies with television, that all-pervasive medium whose marketers like to brag that it is everyone's primary source of news and information. It is also everyone's primary source of bad English. I have frequently demonstrated to my own satisfaction, or to make a point with others, that one can find an example of egregiously incorrect English by tuning in to any TV newscast and paying attention for two or three minutes. I have won a number of bets that way. This is an appalling state of affairs. Each of these mistakes is heard by thousands or millions, and most of those listeners naively believe that what they are hearing is the work of professionals who know what they're doing.

The Canadian Broadcasting Corporation deserves particular criticism in this respect. It's not that the CBC is any worse than any other broadcaster — the reverse is probably true — but that it was created and maintained at public expense to provide a service of high quality. Its news and information programming should be written and spoken in an exemplary manner. My recollection is that it respected this responsibility in its earlier years. I can remember when the CBC was created in 1936. It sounded pretty good, but perhaps I was a bit less critical then.

Over the decades, it has become so lax that I will offer the bet mentioned above with almost as much confidence when the chosen newscast is a CBC one rather than the product of a private operation. I do get a little nervous in the case of a national newscast, and start hoping for an early segment fed in from a local news bureau. And I have an ace in the hole. The title of the 10 P.M. national newscast is *The National. National* is an adjective. I complained when the title was instituted, and kept asking "The National *What?*", but no one answered. Every time *The National* identifies itself it is making an error. Anyway, the decline of standards in English usage is less evident in CBC network news than elsewhere, but a decline it is.

Let's look at just one example. It is a common error to confuse *mitigate,* which means make less severe, and *militate,* which means influence. It's no big deal to look up the words and fix the distinction in your mind, but the error is propagated and perpetuated by political leaders and broadcasters who are too indifferent or lazy or stupid to do that simple thing. (I am writing this paragraph just minutes after hearing the host of a CBC Newsworld national TV program commit the offence, and am in a mild rage.) I do not get terribly upset by someone committing an uncommon error, but insist that there is no excuse for such people committing *common* errors.

Some of television's top talkers don't make great role models. These people have an enormous influence on the speech habits of the public, and I don't think they care much about the damage they do. Larry King, for example, is one of the most successful interview-show hosts anywhere. His nightly hour-long program on the Cable News Network (CNN) is watched by millions of people around the world. He is fairly articulate, but, for someone of his potential influence, his English is atrocious. It seems not to matter. He has had a long and lucrative career doing the same work in radio (which he still does), and was an instant and enduring success on TV, apparently without ever needing to improve his language skills. He often discusses "heenyous" crimes, and he reports on one "phenomena" after another. Just a few days before I wrote this, King did a show with the veteran TV newscaster David Brinkley, and it was a mistake on his part. Brinkley was so well-spoken that the exchanges sounded like Hamlet's conversation with the gravedigger. Still, you can be pretty sure which of the two is better known and better paid in the 1990s, and I suspect that King's popularity is not so much despite his linguistic shortcomings as because of them; that his listeners feel comfortable with someone whose speech is as poor as theirs.

Another of the major mouths who is in line for some criticism is Johnny Carson, whose career I have followed since he was the host of a daytime game show called *Who Do You Trust?* (not *Whom Do You Trust?*), in the 1950s. Carson, in his earlier days of fame as host of television's *The Tonight Show*, was given to reminding people that he was a college graduate. He did that less and less often as the years went by, and a good thing, too. I jumped on Carson in the first column I wrote for *Books in Canada*, for that reason. Years earlier I had heard him stumble over the distinction between *lay* and *lie* and make an honest effort to correct himself, but eventually he settled down and went on getting it wrong every time without a qualm. It is now a lost cause. Carson might have helped, but obviously decided he couldn't be bothered.

There are articulate and careful TV talkers. Alistair Cooke, William Buckley, Edwin Newman, David Brinkley, Robert MacNeil, to name a few, but they don't grab the ratings. (I once heard MacNeil say *try and* about fifty times during a single TV panel discussion, but forgave him.)

I am cursed with an editor's eye and ear. Misspellings and solecisms leap from the printed page to jar my nerves; errors in speech set my dentures on edge. This particular sensitivity has some professional value, but it can be a curse. I am fond of music, but my perception of pitch is ludicrously poor, and I am grateful for that weakness every time I see one of my musician friends shudder at the occasional clinker in a performance I am finding quite enjoyable. They are put off; I shrug it off. Yet some of these same people, when I complain about a grammatical error committed by a paid writer, say such things as "Well, what's the difference? It's easy enough to figure out what he meant", and it doesn't avail me much to say a sour note is a sour note, whether in music or in English.

I writhe and groan in front of the TV set, and when I am foolish enough to read in bed, a bad night is inevitable. There is plenty of good material to be read in bed — Gibbon, for example — but most of it seems to come in unwieldy tomes. I have a record I treasure, an old LP produced in Sweden, that immortalized the final concert of a festival of high-school orchestras. I take every opportunity to play it for my musician friends and ask them if they would like a tape of it to go to sleep by every night.

The difference is, of course, that most of the music we are exposed to is not that bad, but most of the writing is. I don't know why.

You won't find many technical terms in this book. I don't know many. That doesn't distress or embarrass me greatly. I think it is important that some of the basic terminology be taught in grade school. Once learned, much of it can be more or less forgotten by anyone who is not planning to teach English. Knowing the names for the various parts of speech — nouns, verbs, adjectives, and the like — is essential, but I don't know what *pluperfect* means, and it is a long time since I've cared. What is important to me is that I once knew, and I hope that at that time I learned to use it — the tense, not the word — correctly. It's useful to be told the difference between a participle and a gerund, and to understand what that difference is, but, since you can look it up at any time, I don't think it's too important that you remember the definition of each term, unless you are a teacher. What does matter is grasping the import of the rules, so that you will know, whether you can quote one or not, when you are on thin ice.

I recall an incident from Grade 10 English. The teacher picked one student for each tense. We were given a verb and all sent to the blackboard and instructed to write the first-person singular version for our assigned tense. The given verb was *drink*. I do not remember the name of my assigned tense, and am not curious enough to look it up. What I know is that I wrote, correctly, "I am drunk". My tense was low on the list, and the teacher began at the top to read and evaluate the entries. When she came to mine, she blushed attractively and started stammering apologies for forcing me to write a statement that (at that time) was not true. I suppose she feared that I would tell my parents that she had conned me into confessing to a sin I wasn't guilty of, or something of that sort. I was sufficiently amused to tell my parents, and they were amused. The incident came to mind decades later, when I was visiting Mexico and apologizing to a host for some minor indiscretion. I said "*Soy borracho*", and did not realize until too late that I should have said "*Estoy borracho*", which means I am drunk right now. The former phrase means I am always drunk, which is not entirely true. English is not the only language with difficult verbs.

The thought that lingered with me after the school experience was that the teacher had not carefully considered her choice of a verb for the exercise. *Confuse* might have been a better one. At any rate, they did a good job of hammering that stuff into us, and the effects lingered long after the technical terms were forgotten.

I don't think any serious reader of mature years wants the language to stand still while we all adhere slavishly to the dictates of some dog-eared relic of our schooldays, but I do think it would be reasonable to ask that people be required to have some idea of what the rules are before they start to ignore them.

James J. Kilpatrick, a veteran U.S. journalist and the author of *The Writer's Art,* had some words for would-be writers who have the inclination to barge into the profession (and probably have been encouraged by their teachers to do so) without even a rudimentary knowledge of the tools of their trade. He pointed out that Pablo Picasso spent no less than fifteen years practising representational art before he started doing the kind of work he became best known for. In other words, he became damn' good at drawing people with one nose and two eyes before he started drawing them with one eye and two noses. To put it still another way, you have to learn to walk before you can dance.

I try, but find it difficult, to avoid judging people simply by the way they write. There are, after all, other criteria. I don't expect everyone to write well, but I do expect paid writers to, and I expect such professional people as doctors, lawyers, and politicians to have some grasp of the language, since it is of primary importance that they be able to communicate ideas among themselves and with us, but an alarming number of them are frighteningly deficient in language skills. When I was writing for *Books in Canada,* most of my criticism was directed at the writing of professional communicators, who were the source of most of the horrible examples quoted in those columns. Now, the experience of being exposed to many thousands of efforts at writing by people who might be expected to have been trained to express themselves clearly and carefully has been devastating. For example, I find it difficult to decide how much attention I should pay to an engineer who is expounding on the relative merits of "flourescent" and "incandesent" lighting at a computer workstation. These misspellings were not typing errors. They remained consistent throughout his exposition. The man simply did not know how to spell these words — and many others — although they were terms commonly used in his field of expertise.

I was talking about rules at the beginning of this chapter. There are many rules. Indeed, there are many rulebooks, and their authors do not invariably agree among themselves. A simple answer to the right-or-wrong question might often depend on which authority was being consulted. *Rules* isn't the best word. We're not talking baseball here. I would prefer to speak of conventions and guidelines, but people expect rules, and I'll continue to use the term.

In recent years, I have done some work as a consultant to people who are not professional writers — although they are anything but illiterate — but are required in their work to produce writing that appears professional. They usually expect a simple and direct answer when they ask what is right or wrong, and become impatient when the answer is, for example, "It depends...".

There *are* things that are just plain wrong, and some of them are odd enough to require a rule that should be followed without argument. Many people (most people, I sometimes think) are unaware that the contraction of *you are* is *you're*, not *your*, although it should be obvious to anyone who thinks about it that the one with the apostrophe is the contraction, and the other one is the possessive pronoun. When it comes to the pandemic confusion between *it's* and *its*, the distinction is not so obvious. A rule is needed. Anyone might be forgiven for thinking that if you want the possessive of *it*, you should add an apostrophe and an S to it (although the same person would be unlikely to write "he's" or "him's" instead of "his"). *Its* is in the same category as *his*, and *it's* is the contraction for *it is*. That's the rule, and it's easier just to remember it than to think about it, or so one would expect. I knew a reporter who had a BA in English from Queen's University, who had a full career in newspaper work, and who reached retirement age without ever grasping either the *you're/your* distinction or the fact that the possessive is *yours*, not "your's". Every day I see "their's" and "her's" and the like in print. Even worse is the use of *'s* to form the plural. The authors of signs, posters, and menus are among the worst offenders in this as well as in the ridiculous misuse of quotation marks. Here's a line I copied from a menu:

"Your missing something if you haven't tried our 'home-made' pie's and cake's!!!"

Good grief!

Much of the time the question should not be what is right or wrong, but what is appropriate for the circumstances, and that brings up the question of style. There are umpteen "correct" ways of saying things. The choice can be narrowed if you establish the circumstances under which you are writing or speaking. You determine who you are (or what role you're playing), who your audience is, and what medium you're using, and then the choices become considerably narrowed.

Shakespeare did not have to follow rules, because there weren't any to speak of when he was working. Indeed, when the rules were written, his work frequently served as a model.

When he had Antony speak of Brutus's turning against Caesar as "the most unkindest cut of all", the double superlative was out of step with contemporary usage, and I suppose it was a breach of a then unwritten rule. Anyway, he was writing dialogue, not a scholarly essay, and maybe that's what Antony did say. People said all kinds of odd things that week. I have never been able to understand why Caesar lapsed into Latin and said "*Et tu, Brute?*", although up to that point he had demonstrated that his English was excellent. (After all, he had quite recently returned from a trip to England.)

When people did start codifying rules, they modelled them on Latin, which, being a dead language, offered the convenience of a model that, unlike English, was not evolving every day. There was, I have been told, little other advantage to trying to make English fit Latin-type rules, but that's the way it went. This is just one of the reasons for taking issue with some of the things we have been taught.

At some time in the mid-1980s I was covering a preview screening of a major TVOntario educational television series. (TVO is a child of the Ontario government's ministry of education, born in the

1960s.) We were provided with scripts, and I noticed, on the opening page of the narration, perhaps a half-dozen grammatical errors, which were faithfully read by the narrator. I was chatting with the public relations person who was promoting the series, and she asked me what I had been doing lately. I said that I had been doing some editing. Being a TV person, she thought I meant film editing, and became confused when I said no, I meant text editing. I explained that, for example, had I been given a chance to look at the very script we had in our hands, I could have saved the educational TV arm of Ontario the embarrassment of committing grammatical gaffes in this supposedly educational program. She was unable to recognize the mistakes I pointed out, and obviously couldn't see that any of this mattered. I mentioned the errors to two or three other TVO people present, none of whom showed the slightest interest.

That was probably the most discouraging single indication I've ever seen of the uncomprehending indifference to the importance of language skills that pervades not only the field of communications but that of education.

A new form of written communication exploded in the 1980s, nourished by the spread of personal computers. Electronic bulletin board services (BBSs) provide anyone having access to even the simplest computer with the means of exchanging messages with other computer users virtually anywhere in the world. Most of these messages are public, and can be read by anyone subscribing to the BBS that carries them. A local system I subscribe to, Rose Media in Toronto, gives me access to almost 6,000 international special-interest conferences on every conceivable subject from astronomy to zoology. Every day, about 60,000 new messages are posted in these conferences. This is one of the large systems, but there are some even more massive.

I'll be talking about this more in a later chapter, but the phenomenon had so much influence on this book that it needs a mention here. The BBS networks offer the opportunity to examine the writing of a tremendous variety of people — people of all ages (from about ten up), people of all educational backgrounds and vocations, and, above all, people who are trying, often with great difficulty, to communicate with one another by writing and reading. By and large, they are making a terrible botch of it.

Before live TV coverage of the proceedings of the House of Commons was begun, there were years of argument about the effects it might have on Parliament and its members. The chief concern was that the MPs would "go Hollywood" and start performing as entertainers rather than as politicians (as if there were any fundamental difference between the two).

During all that time of indecision, I didn't hear a word of debate about the possible effects on *viewers*. Today, I cannot perceive any significant deterioration (or improvement) in the behaviour of the MPs, but I am deeply disturbed about how these broadcasts may be affecting the people who watch them.

The danger lies in the possibility that impressionable viewers of all ages might believe that the language they hear being spoken in the august precincts of the Green Chamber is good English. It rarely is. Most of our elected representatives (I can speak only about the Anglophones among them) mangle our language almost as viciously as do sports commentators, and probably in a more damaging way.

What's at issue here is not merely sloppiness of style. It's the wanton destruction of our chief means of letting each other — or ourselves — know what is on our minds. In an essay on the decline of the art of editing, *Time* magazine recently came to the conclusion that "proper usage matters because writing is thought and clear writing is essential for clear thinking". *Time* is certainly not without sin, but that at least was an expression of good intentions. The true enemy is not the writer who makes a mistake. It is the writer who doesn't give a damn, who is ignorant of his ignorance or simply is comfortable in it, who is unaware of or indifferent to his destructive power. He is guilty of perversion, and if he thinks that is a nasty thing to say about him, he should look it up in his dictionary, which is a book designed to help him with his diction.

Writers who won't take the trouble to maintain distinctions in meaning are destroying our ability to communicate with each other. A financial-page columnist tells us we will have "less dollars" to spend next year. Quite possibly next year he will be telling us we will have "fewer money" to spend the following year. What does he care? He's too busy dreaming up such phrases as *negative growth* so he won't have to say *decline.*

Something that is continual either never stops or keeps recurring forever. Something that is continuous goes non-stop from start to finish. This is another distinction the lesser lexicographers are abandoning, and in this case perhaps they're justified by the continual misuse of *continuous* by so many writers.

There remain, however, some frequently ignored distinctions that are worth trying to preserve. There are, we are too often reminded, writers who need to be reminded often that while a long drive on a tortuous road can be a torturous experience for a driver, *tortuous* and *torturous* have different meanings, as have *contemptuous* and *contemptible, ingenious* and *ingenuous, obtuse* and *abstruse, uninterested* and *disinterested.* These distinctions should be obvious, but I've seen one or both words in each of those pairs misused for the other, in print, within one week. In view of that, is there any use in arguing further — or farther?

CHAPTER 2

All the News Unfit for Print

It's said, and said most often on TV, that surveys show most people in Canada and the United States rely on television as their primary source of news. That certainly bothered me during the decades I was living mostly on the avails of newspaper work, such as they were, but doubtless it is true, and I am one of those people.

"News" is seldom clearly defined in such reports, and the surveys (to some of which I have been a respondent) are not precise in their questions. What I call news is what's happened since the last time I looked, and in those terms there's really no contest. I subscribe to some newspapers, but when they arrive at my door they rarely contain surprises. Even if one has a real scoop, the story will have been broken on TV already by someone who has seen a copy of the paper hot off the press. The most I ask of the papers is that they give me more detailed information about events I have been aware of for many hours, and such information, however valuable, doesn't qualify as "news" by my definition. It has already become background.

What is relevant here is that either medium gives us news that is badly written. I don't know if newspaper news is as badly written as television news, but I suspect that it's a tossup. If this is so, it is partly because many of the people writing for newspapers nowadays acquired their language skills by watching TV, not by reading good writing.

A few years ago, for example, the author of a piece intended to advise TV viewers on making the most of the opportunity to watch the full coverage of Parliamentary debates provided on cable television told her readers that MPs sometimes express approval by shouting "Here, here!". I submit that that writer was not a reader. That wasn't a reader's mistake, it was a listener's mistake. Anyone who has ever peeked into *Hansard* (as one might assume a writer would do before attempting to instruct us on watching TV coverage of Parliament) knows how to spell *Hear, hear*. Spelling by ear is not a good practice for someone who writes for print.

Another serious problem is the result of the fact that wherever news writing is taught, be it in school or on the job, there is always emphasis on "tight writing", and somehow this has gotten out of hand. Brevity, though it may be the soul of wit, is not necessarily the soul of clear communication. For example, when a reporter tells us that a move by the city's housing committee was "welcomed by homeless advocates", we have to guess that he is referring to those public-spirited citizens who try to help "the homeless", and not, as his words suggest, lawyers who have no place to live. I listened with some curiosity to a social scientist from an American university who said she had been a "rape advocate" for many years. Had she said she had functioned as an advocate for victims of rape, that would have been fine, but what she said suggests that she had been speaking out in favour of rape.

Let's look at a couple of words that have been violated by the news media in the name of tight writing. We are often warned by our ever-protective anchorpersons that the report we are about to see contains some "graphic" footage, to which we might not wish to expose our loved ones — or even ourselves. Now, simply and primarily, *graphic*, as an adjective, means giving a clear and effective picture. It used to be most commonly used in relation to language. A written description that evoked a strong visual image would be called graphic. But what our guardian angel at the anchor desk is telling us is that the *pictures* we are about to see are clear and effective. Why, in God's name, would the newscast be using them if they were *not* graphic?

What is meant here is not that the pictures are graphic. What is meant is that they are graphic representations of something that might offend delicate sensibilities. To say only that they are graphic, and to misuse the word frequently for this purpose, is to begin to undermine its value as a real word.

In a similar vein, we are sometimes warned, at the beginning of a news item or a program, that it contains "explicit" material. The applicable meaning of *explicit* in this context would have to be "fully and clearly expressed or demonstrated, leaving nothing to the imagination". Once again, what is wrong with being explicit when providing a news and information service on television? I, for one, would want such services to be explicit — and graphic. If I am told that an upcoming program, or segment thereof, contains graphic language and explicit photography, I might say that it's about time. But if I am told it contains language and pictures that I might choose not to watch, I would appreciate the thoughtful warning.

Neither *graphic* nor *explicit* held any connotation of offensiveness until very recently, and they shouldn't.

A news report that began "Workers idled through a layoff" stopped me cold. What else would they be doing? How could they work through a layoff? It took me a moment to realize that the writer had committed the sin of using the verb *idle* in the transitive sense of make idle. He meant that they were idle, or unemployed, because of a layoff, not that they had been unemployed or inactive during a layoff. There's no justification for this use. Teachers and editors who stress the importance of tight writing are often lax in warning of its pitfalls, one of which is the temptation to coin new usages. I'm sure this writer was striving for tightness, but what he achieved was ambiguity.

The aspiring reporter who considers niceties of language unimportant fails to realize that he is jeopardizing one of his most valuable assets: his credibility. The sports reporter who tells us that this team "eked out a win over" that team does not know the meaning of the word *eke*. Is it not possible, then, that he also doesn't know the score?

The papers are forever telling us that so-and-so "died of an apparent heart attack". Either he died of a heart attack or he didn't. If it seemed that the cause of death was a heart attack, then he died, apparently of a heart attack. I suppose that if it appeared to one that one was having a heart attack, that might frighten one to death. That would be dying of an apparent heart attack. But I don't think that's what reporters mean when they use the phrase, and, since they can't say what they mean, I wonder whether the guy is, in fact, dead.

Possible sometimes vies with *apparent* for misuse of this type. We hear of people dying of possible heart attacks (or strokes or whatever), too, and that's just as silly. One station went for a full twenty-four-hour cycle of newscasts reporting of a particular fire that "a possible electrical problem is believed to be the cause". While I was working on this chapter I caught a newscast in which a wanted burglary suspect was described as "wearing a possible moustache". That's in the same class as a missing person who was described as having "long brown hair and eyes".

More than twenty-four hours after a Supreme Court decision on the constitution was published, a reporter informed us that "it's hard to say who was the clear winner here". I made a note of it, but I remain uncertain whether it was the result of plain stupidity or of sloppy writing. It was obvious, seconds after Chief Justice Bora Laskin began speaking, that the very essence of the news story was that there was no clear winner (between the contending provincial governments on the one side and the federal government on the other). I refuse to believe that any professional journalist could have failed, by the following afternoon, to grasp that fact. It must have been sloppy writing, spawned by the currently endemic journalistic addiction to circumlocution.

It's hard to say is one of the many cop-out phrases favoured by journalists who cannot bring themselves to say "I don't know". Such dodges, used too often, become catch-phrases that tend to be thrown into use even when inappropriate. Probably what the reporter was trying to say was that the story was confusing because, while there was no clear winner, both sides were claiming victory. That could be said in a dozen ways; she chose none of them.

Or perhaps she was trying to say that eventually one side might prove to have won out, but it was not yet clear to her which side that would be.

What she did tell us, in effect, was that there *was* a clear winner, but she didn't know who it was, and that's nonsense.

Sources say is a relatively new abomination in the cop-out lexicon. The use of *source* to refer to a cautious blabbermouth is a hoary journalistic tradition. I don't like it, but I've become inured to lines like "a source in the Prime Minister's Office says...". It has long been used by responsible reporters to conceal the identity of useful informants, and I have no quarrel with careful use of the dodge. If a reputable journalist tells me that a "source" in the Prime Minister's Office, who has asked not to be identified, has confirmed the opposition leader's statement that a Cabinet shuffle is imminent, I'll pay some attention. But I don't know what *sources say* means. It's a real cop-out. It is never *a source says*; it is always in the plural, as if to reassure us that the reporter has not simply taken the word of one possibly unreliable person but has checked the information with at least one other possibly unreliable person. It turns a questionable practice into an insupportable one, and its use has spread explosively.

In a very few years, it has become commonplace in electronic and even print journalism to hear or read that sources say this or that, with no explanation at all of who these sources might be. The writers are assuming, perhaps correctly, that the word has acquired some magic connotation of reliability in the public mind.

This terminology, which I first noticed in the sleazier media, can now be found in major newspapers and newsmagazines, and heard a dozen times an hour on network television newscasts. I haven't seen any evidence of anyone objecting to it. I think it shows a great contempt for the public, but, in turn, it may be contributing to an increasing public contempt for the news media. Occasionally, you will run across such phrases as *it has been confirmed that* and may not notice that there's no mention of who did the confirming. There are many such tricks, but they aren't tried too often. Somehow, though, practically everyone in the business seems to feel confident of getting away with *sources say,* and this has led to the worst kind of irresponsible sloppiness.

Interviewers who haven't the foggiest idea what the term means are always talking about "begging the question". They can't even agree on how to misuse it. One will accuse his subject of begging the question if the latter seems to be avoiding a direct answer. Another will say: "What you've just told me begs the question 'why did you do it?'."

"Beg the question" is English for *petitio principii.* To use Fowler's simple and clear explanation, it refers to "the fallacy of founding a conclusion on a basis that as much needs to be proved as the conclusion itself". To say that children should obey their parents because their parents know best would be begging the

question. It could be a useful phrase for TV interviewers in particular, but I have yet to hear one use it correctly. However, I once
raised my hat to the intrepid *Globe and Mail* critic Jay Scott for
daring to go against the editorial policy of his employer. A lead
editorial in the paper had contained a flagrant misuse of the term,
so I assumed that such misuse was a matter of policy. Not long
after that, Scott wrote: "The notion that 'sincerity' is what's missing from American politics, the notion that The People can be
trusted to respond to a man who's honest about his innards, elab-
orately begs the question; Hitler, after all, was undeniably sincere,
and he had no trouble expressing his feelings." I fretted at the time
that Scott had placed his job in jeopardy, but he stayed on, continuing to write real good.

I was only a couple of days into my newspaper career when I
misspelled the name of the subject of an obituary. I was told, and
not too gently, "This guy's family probably never saw his name in
print before, and probably never will again, so is it too much to ask
that you spell it right?". I also was reminded that it is courting trouble to get a living person's name wrong. People, even today, do not
like to see either their own or their dear departed's names messed
up. That, however, is not the most important consideration. An
error in spelling a word is bad enough, but an error in spelling a
name is an error in fact. If I write "embarassing" just once, it may be
embarrassing for me, but it is unlikely to change the world much. If
I misspell your name in print, I am creating misinformation about
you that may spread and spread.

I don't think this point is being taught the way it used to be. I've
particularly noticed this in press releases over the decades. There's a
tired old line often spoken by celebrities and, more often, by
would-be celebrities: "I don't care what you say about me, as long
as you spell my name right." Today, a reporter might reply "How in

hell am *I* supposed to spell it right if your press agent can't spell it right?". I can recall a time when the simplest and surest way for an entertainment writer on a newspaper to check the spelling of a performer's name was to look at a press release. That has not been true for some time, and today's newspaper libraries provide an instant nightmare for a reporter or editor on deadline trying to make a fast check on a name.

I think it was during the 1980s that practically all reporters started telling us that "another child has gone missing", or that "the mental patient went missing last Wednesday". The term has been around for a while, but it simply took over fairly recently. I don't think it belongs in written English. "A child is missing" says it, as does "The mental patient disappeared" (or escaped, or whatever he did).

Some of the people I've discussed this with say that if you can *go hunting* then you can *go missing,* and I say that if that's the case it only means that you are a poor shot. If a person went shooting, he went to shoot. If he went missing, he went to miss, and that makes him okay in my book.

Then they tell me that *missing* is descriptive of a condition, and so is *mad,* and if a person can go mad, he can go missing (and, of course, that is sometimes the case). I really don't know what in hell to say to that. If he goes wenching, then he is hunting for a wench, so perhaps if he goes missing he is hunting for a miss. I don't know. Wouldn't it be simpler to say he can't be found, that he has disappeared, that he is inexplicably absent from his habitat, that he ain't been seen around lately, not *no*where, or just that he's *missing?* More recently, reporters have started saying that *things* have gone missing, meaning simply that they were stolen.

For a time I feared that the situation was getting even worse. Some reporters stopped saying that someone "has gone missing" and started saying he "has turned up missing", but, in a way, that's better. That's in a class with Sam Goldwyn's "Include me out" (if Sam Goldwyn did indeed ever say that). It's *cute*. Put it in your book of cute expressions. Don't fret about it.

I've seldom bothered to worry about the language of TV sports commentators. The reason is simple: the language of sports commentators bears so little resemblance to English that I'm not sure any discussion of it belongs here. However, a CBC hockey commentator caught my ear recently with a compound error common enough to warrant some attention.

What the man said was that "both goalies are very similar". *Both* is wrong here. It lumps the goalies together and suggests that, together, they are similar to someone else. Similarity is reciprocal; if A resembles B to some degree, then B resembles A to the same degree. That's two strikes against *both*. *Very* is wrong. *Similar* is not an absolute like *unique*. Sports commentators who say (and, God, do they say it!) *very unique* are wrong because there are no degrees of uniqueness. There can be varying degrees of similarity. However, in this context, one could assume that the similarity was remarkable enough to be remarked on, and the *very* is not really necessary. What the commentator was trying to convey was not that the goalies were similar, but that their styles of play were similar. But, rather than be accused of nitpicking, I'd be willing to let the man say the goalies are similar if he were willing to drop the *both* and the *very*.

It's not uncommon to read that some top-seeded player was an "upset victim in today's play at Wimbledon", but the story will reveal neither what he was upset about nor what he was a victim of. There are many potholes in the road to tight writing, boys and girls. An upset victim is not the same thing as the victim of an upset.

A CBC newscast, dealing with World Cup soccer, contained a reference to "Italy's defeat over Poland".

A wire-service story about Peter Pocklington (remember him?) said "after he tried selling the team, he...". He didn't try selling it. He tried to sell it. Do not ask why this is so. Trust me. It has less to do with infinitives and gerunds than it has to do with the pesky *try* (not quite five columns in the *OED*). To try doing something is to experiment; to try to do something is to make an attempt to do it. The way things are nowadays, a chap might have to try selling vacuum cleaners, and, if he were not to succeed in that enterprise, he might have to try to sell his own vacuum cleaner.

How about this line from a sports report that said some football player had "rebounded from a broken hand"? Whose? I think it meant he had recovered quickly from an injury.

A report on CBC-TV's now-defunct *The Journal* said that someone had emerged from an ordeal "battle-scarred but intact". Neatest trick of the day, perhaps.

A headline in a major weekly newspaper published in the Toronto area said that "One in four in Metro Toronto are illiterate". The error is repeated in the caption of an adjacent photograph. It also appears in the text of the article, in company with at least a dozen other errors.

Here is the opening paragraph:

> The statistics are disheartening, scary. One out of four people in Metro over the age of 15 are illiterate. Twenty percent cannot read or write well enough to understand a newspaper, a street sign or fill out a job application.

I guess I are that one. Possibly I can write well enough to understand a newspaper, whatever that means, but I cannot read well enough to understand this one. I don't even understand the arithmetic. In my book, one in four works out to twenty-five percent, but since the writer doesn't say twenty percent of what, who knows?

Enough of being flippant. There is a terrible irony here. Obviously, the reporter, while he is bemoaning the situation that he is attempting to describe, is unaware (as are his editors) that he is writing execrably.

Presumably he is referring to what is now called "functional illiteracy", which is a serious enough problem. More troubling, though, is the percentage of professional writers and speakers who, to use the same terminology, could claim at best to be "functionally literate", but who cannot choose words and place them in sentences in a way that clearly and accurately conveys the information they are being paid to impart. That percentage, although I know of no studies to support my guess, must be seventy-five or higher.

Another thing that is happening is that the few good editors left are becoming contaminated by being exposed to such massive doses of bad usage that they become confused about standards that once were clear to them. This is a serious occupational hazard. Editors, no matter what anyone says, are people, and all people are potential victims of language pollution.

The person who is functionally illiterate, while his inability to comprehend the significance of the letters S-T-O-P on an hexagonal red sign might result in someone's death, is not as great a menace to society as is the paid communicator making his daily contribution to the cataclysmic erosion of English that is accompanying the so-called information explosion.

Correctness does not always ensure clarity. If a reporter visiting a university campus tells us that the students are "revolting", we need to know whether he is stating a fact (they are rebelling) or voicing an opinion (they are disgusting). *Revolting* can mean either, and should be avoided if there is any possibility of misunderstanding.

If, however, the reporter intends the second meaning and elaborates by saying they are making him "nauseous", he is guilty of an increasingly (and sickeningly) common misuse of *nauseous*, which means nauseating, or nauseated. He could just say *sick*, but he's probably one of those persons who say *presently* when they mean now.

This represents the other side of the tight writing coin. This fellow (he's on all the newscasts and writes for all the papers) doesn't *invariably* say *presently* when he means now. He would not use *at this moment in time*, because he knows it's a redundancy (all moments are in time), but he'll take any opportunity to use *at this point in time*, a phrase he finds satisfyingly pompous. He'll probably soon join the ranks of those who have started to say *technological advancements* instead of advances. *Advancement* is arguably permissible in that context, but its chief attraction seems to be its extra syllable. No communicator who hopes to be regarded as a pundit can afford to pass up a suitably sesquipedalian substitute for a short word. Consider the respected broadcast journalist John Chancellor, who, in his later years, has stopped using *describe* in favour of *characterize.*

A news-service report on plans for future missions of the U.S. space shuttle described how an astronaut equipped with a personal jet-propulsion device will leave the shuttle to "jet over to a malfunctioning satellite designed to study the sun and fix it". Laugh if you will, but bear in mind that that same writer's sloppiness some other time could result in your being misinformed in some way that could have serious consequences to you. The mistake was ludicrous, but not funny.

That example also brings to mind the fix *fix* is in. It's only recently that lexicographers have stopped affixing the label *colloq.* to the use of *fix* in the sense of repair, but that use is fixed in the minds of most of us. While we still may fix our eyes on something, when we speak of fixing an object we are speaking of repairing it, not fastening it in place. When you ask a repairman to fix your television set, you don't expect him to nail it to the floor. We have *repair* and *mend*. We didn't need *fix* to replace them, but by putting it to that use we have made it useless as a short, sharp, accurate way of saying something for which we now lack an unequivocal word.

Another reporter spoke of the government's having "dispensed with the constitution". That is patently ridiculous; we knew the government hadn't got rid of the constitution. But suppose there had been a debate going on in the Commons about, say, a proposed increase in the gasoline tax, and the same reporter suddenly told us that the government had dispensed with the gasoline tax. What would we make of that?

A reporter on CBC-TV's national newscast said this of a man whose attempt to rob a bank was foiled: "He never got any money." Were that true, I suppose it would explain why the poor fellow was driven to try robbery. The use of *never* for *didn't* is a vulgar error of the lowest sort. I have long since abandoned the hope that the CBC would one day take seriously its responsibility to offer us a model of good English, but I still wasn't prepared to hear that line.

Possibly Humpty Dumpty, the classic arbiter of the meaning of words, was manning the rewrite desk at Broadcast News the day that two consecutive items raised interesting questions of diction. One, referring to the *Ocean Ranger* tragedy of 1982, said "the oil rig slipped into the gelid Atlantic". The other reported that Menachem Begin, then prime minister of Israel, "virulently opposes the plan".

To object to these uses comes close to nitpicking, but I think they're worth arguing about. *Gelid* does, indeed, mean extremely cold or icy, and I presume that that's what Humpty Dumpty chose that it mean. It also means refreshingly cold, however, and was hardly appropriate in that sense. Furthermore, *gelid* is not an everyday word, and it makes many readers think of *gelatin*, with which it shares a common ancestor.

Broadcast News began as an arm of the Canadian Press news service. It furnished the lifeblood of "rip-and-read" newscasters, and its reports can be seen printed out on the news channels of many cable-television services. It is no place for fancy synonyms. The writer obviously meant icy, and that's the word he should have used.

There may have been some justification for the quoted use of *virulently*. While *virulent* primarily means poisonous, it can also be used to denote extreme bitterness. It's a strong word, though, and it has a connotation of evil that brings its use in this context under suspicion of editorializing. *Vehemently* would have served very well in this context. Perhaps the writer did mean virulently, but anyone who would use *gelid* when he meant icy must be suspected of being a show-off who probably spends far too much of his time in search of what Fowler scornfully calls "elegant variations".

And, speaking of alternatives, the adjective *alternate* means occurring by turns, or every other. It is not an acceptable alternative for the adjective *alternative*.

A news story widely circulated during a royal tour reported that "the Queen chatted amicably" with somebody on her recent visit to the west coast. That's hardly news, but it illustrates the point that when reporters are forced to write at length about newsless events, they are more likely than usual to say something stupid.

When you chat with someone, you are, by definition, making light and pleasant conversation in a friendly manner, and that's all there is to it. You cannot chat in a hostile manner.

There remains the question of whether the Queen was indeed conversing amicably rather than amiably. These days, one cannot rely on writers to make such fine distinctions. *Amicable* refers to something done with good will. *Amiable* refers to a person's nature or expression or attitude. It is entirely possible that the Queen was inwardly seething with rage at the necessity of conversing amiably, in which case she would not have been conversing amicably, although she might have given the impression that she was. Amiability is readily observable by a reporter. Amicability is not. "Chatted amicably" is a double fault.

Then there was the reporter who informed us that "the bomb was defused before it exploded".

It's not likely that anyone would spend much time wondering how it came to pass that the bomb exploded despite having been defused. We know it did not explode. We know the reporter should have said "before it could explode" or some such.

Suppose, though, that he had said something like "the bank robber was arrested before he made his getaway". (Someone *did* say that.) That's the same construction, and, in this case, we would have to assume that the robber had been arrested and then escaped, because that's what the writer said.

I don't think it would be proper to dismiss any of the above as nit-picking. I doubt that there has ever been an entire news program, local or network, devoid of such gaffes, and whether they are caused by carelessness or ignorance doesn't matter. They are all detrimental to the usefulness of the English language. In fairness to broadcast journalists, it must be admitted that while they are not required to spell or punctuate, they are required to be able to pronounce words and to blow-dry their hair, skills that are not demanded of print journalists. I do suggest that they be held as accountable for their sins as are print journalists for their unfortunately less ephemeral ones.

CHAPTER 3

Anything for a Buck

Around the middle of this century, there was a lively spurt of public debate about an advertising campaign that claimed "Winston tastes good, like a cigarette should".

It should, of course, have been "*as* a cigarette should".

Today, there would be hardly a murmur. There was a bit of fuss when some Kraft product was claimed to be "more cheesier", but it didn't amount to much. Advertisers can get away with much more than they once could. This may be disappointing to them, since the controversy certainly didn't hurt Winston.

And, if the Winston ad were to be attacked today, its creator would have to look no farther than the *RH-II* to find authoritative support for the use of *like* as a conjunction.

This reflects two ills: the deterioration of standards of English usage, which is reflected as clearly in the later dictionaries as it is anywhere else, and the deliberate, shameless maltreatment of the language by the advertising industry. I've always thought, and still do, that advertising people are a pretty smart breed and know exactly what they're doing when they mess around with the language.

ANYTHING FOR A BUCK

The critic John Simon says that *plus* is a mathematical term and has no place in written English. Lacking Mr. Simon's well-known arrogance, I would not go that far. *Plus* can be many things, but a conjunction is not one of them. Even the *RH-II* labels that use as "informal", which is, for that dictionary, a pretty strong condemnation. I would make it a hanging offence to use the word as a conjunction, although I'm sure there are ad men who would rather go to the gallows than relinquish the misuse of *plus*, given its powerful connotation of MORE, MORE, MORE. If intentional abuse of the language will sell soap, they'll do it.

So we have advertisers saying: "For just $39.95, we'll send you the complete kit, PLUS you get a year's supply of navel-lint solvent and a set of steak knives FOR FREE!!" (Please note the *for free*. Advertising copy writers are forbidden to say anything is free; they must say it is "for free".) An oft-played commercial for AT&T long-distance telephone services in the United States used *for free* ("Call now and we'll switch you back for free") four times in one minute. (Another AT&T commercial boasts that "The longer you talk, the more you save". It might have claimed more accurately that the more you spend, the greater the discount, but obviously that would not have been as beguiling. And I have a clipping somewhere of an ad for "a service being trialed by Bell Canada".)

The most egregious example of this use of *plus* I have spotted is in *Encyclopædia Britannica* advertising. Surely one might expect the purveyors of such a venerable educational resource to be more careful.

Despite what Simon says, *plus* does serve some purposes beyond the world of mathematics. It is easier, and as correct, to say *plus* instead of *in addition to*. In the example above, eliminating "you get" makes the sentence acceptable (apart from the *for free*, which is unpardonable in any context). The upshot of the incessant misuse is that even usually well-spoken people nowadays pollute their conversation with it.

To return to the *Britannica*: not long ago I received, from one Norm Woods of the Britannica Home Library Service, a piece of promotional mail that began: "Dear Friend: As a preferred Britannica customer I am pleased to announce a special preview offer on the new HISTORY OF THE 20TH CENTURY. For the very first time you can read about every aspect of life in our world from 1900 to the present." This, apart from being just plain stupid, contains an excellent example of the misguided modifier. Perhaps the genial Mr. Woods (who, by the way, is no dear friend of mine, and has no business calling me one of his) is a preferred Britannica customer. I don't think that's what he meant to say, but that's what he did say. His second sentence is pure nonsense.

My feelings about the *Britannica* (which I once saw spelled with two Ts and one N in one of the company's promotions) are coloured by my bizarre experience in purchasing my own copy. I had long revered the publication, and was ill-prepared for the kind of hucksterism that is employed in its marketing. In 1974, no longer having a staffer's access to any newspaper library, I decided the time had come when I must buy an encyclopedia of my own. I found a phone number in an ad, called it, and asked the price. I was told a salesman would visit me. I said that I did not want to be sold, I simply wanted to buy, but no, this was not the way it worked. So the salesman came to the tiny garret I rented as an office, and began his scripted sales pitch. I broke in and said again that I was prepared to write a cheque, and asked how much. Quite disturbed, he rewound and started his pitch again. This happened several times, and became as amusing as it was exasperating. He was simply incapable of deviating from his memorized spiel, even when I told him he could either sell me the goddam books or get out.

This is not really a digression. The point is that the poor man was like a TV announcer without his TelePrompTer. He had no communications skills of his own. I might have expected this, since it fits the style of a company that sees nothing wrong in having its product — an educational tool, I remind you — advertised with no respect for the English language.

I would be less critical of ad writers were they to exercise their cunning without eroding the language to the extent they do. The incessant drumming of their prose on the ears of TV audiences and the eyes of readers of all ages has a detrimental effect on the lifelong process of learning English. (It's worth noting that one of the basic concepts of the long-running and much-lauded *Sesame Street* TV series is to use the techniques of TV advertising as educational tools.)

I entertain the suspicion that the most thoughtful and painstaking writing today is done by people who are interested more in misleading than in informing their readers or listeners. In addition to ad writers, I would include public relations consultants, polemicists, demagogues, and high-level political speech writers in this group. I don't think ordinary politicians should be included. Few of them are capable of good writing, no matter how base their motives. Advertising copy writers, though, remain at the top of my list. As I've said, they are, for the most part, canny characters with a good grasp of the language, and I do stand in some awe of their expertise in twisting words to achieve their often nefarious ends.

From the way they talk to us, I perceive that advertisers are contemptuous of us, so I have no hesitation in proclaiming my contempt for them. When an advertiser tells me there are two scoops of raisins in a package of Kellogg's Raisin Bran, he is taking me for a fool. There is no commonly accepted definition of the size of either a scoop or a package, and the claim is meaningless. This cereal comes also in individual-serving packages, which really makes me wonder about the size of a "scoop". There have been many commercials using this slogan. I can spot them all instantly, and they top the long list of ads that will actually lead me to go to the trouble of switching channels, thanking Providence for the remote control. Anyway, I don't like raisins in my food.

I do eat Kellogg's Special K, and was irritated for years by the claim that "one ounce of Special K with four ounces of milk is a good dietary source of protein". I wondered what 1.5 ounces of cereal with six ounces of milk would be. I also wondered, since I was eating the stuff, how it could be anything other than a dietary source. I eventually discovered that "good dietary source" is bureaucratese, not English. To make that claim, the manufacturer must be able to demonstrate that the combination described contains a specified dose of proteins. If it had more, it could be claimed to be an "excellent" dietary source; less would qualify it as only "fair". No doubt there are other governmental regulations that account for some (relatively little, I imagine) of the silly language used by advertisers. Who knows? Maybe somewhere there is a regulation that defines a scoop as X% of a package.

When writers of advertising are obfuscatory, I pay them the compliment of assuming that they are doing it on purpose. They must believe that if they can convey an impression without saying something that actually *means* something, they have achieved their purpose. The Eveready people claim that one of their batteries "contains as much as five times less [mercury] than all the others". Another of their batteries, they say, "gives you more power than you pay for". I haven't the foggiest idea what either of these claims means, but how could anyone fail to be impressed by something that offers you as much as five times less of a contaminant. I wonder if there is a raisin bran that offers as little as five times more? As for getting more power than I pay for, I like the idea, but the claim doesn't make any sense. If they mean the product delivers more power than does Brand X, for the same price, they should say so. Also, I cannot quickly grasp the significance of claims that something is priced "up to 20% less", and I am not overly impressed with the Players' Club Card advertisements that tell me "they automatically take 25% off the meal". I would much prefer that they take twenty-five percent off the bill.

Much advertising copy is so downright silly that it's difficult even to get annoyed about it.

A Molson Canadian commercial tells us that "In Canada, to be successful, a beer must be clean, clear, crisp, and cold". I'll buy the first three, but by what stretch of the imagination can a brewer legitimately claim that his product is inherently cold? But *cold* is catching. Old Vienna is advertised as "clear, cold, real-life beer". What is the opposite of real-life beer? Imaginary beer? Another beer "tastes less filling". That's even sillier. Are we going to have butter that tastes less fattening, maybe, or arsenic that tastes less poisonous? A testimonial for Pears shampoo says that it "makes my hair feel soft, manageable, and very shiny". I can stretch my imagination to allow the possibility that hair can feel manageable, but I balk at the suggestion that it can feel shiny.

A confection called Rolo claims to be "the most delicious candy ever made". How could anyone take such a claim seriously? How could anyone make such a claim legally? I've always thought that advertisers are supposed to be able to support their claims with research. I suppose that *delicious* connotes a subjective judgment, but I don't see how that could be used as a cop-out here, since the judgment is not attributed to anyone.

A coffee advertising slogan says the product is "hand-picked by Juan Valdez". That is simply absurd — so absurd, I suppose, that the sponsor feels sure that no one would challenge it.

The same goes for "It's the way we play", a slogan wedged into many commercials for Labatt's beer. It has no relevance to any context in which it's used.

A woman in a TV commercial for disposable diapers tells us that having a baby was the ultimate experience of her life. One must assume that she is speaking from the grave.

A blurb for McCain frozen French-fried potatoes depicts a

precocious brat saying "I just ate the last one". He is seen holding
the last one in his hand, and then proceeding to eat it. Were
he truly precocious, he would have said "I am about to eat the
last one".

Reebok claims to be "the number one aerobic shoe". I can find
no definition of *aerobic* that would justify applying the adjective to
a shoe, although I would accept "aerobic exercise shoe".

Coca-Cola in the late 1980s changed its traditional recipe. In
response to a public outcry (which I suspect was not entirely spon-
taneous), the company reinstated its old recipe under the new
brand name Coca-Cola Classic. In 1991, it introduced "Caffeine-
free Coca-Cola Classic...the Real Thing". How can it be the classic
without caffeine? And just what do they mean (in this or any of
their other advertising) by "the real thing"? It makes as much sense
to me as "Pizza Hut and nuthin' but", a statement I'm sure could
not be refuted in court.

There is more than one dentifrice on the market that claims it
"fights tartar above the gum line". Every time I see that claim, I
wonder whether it applies to the lower or upper jaw. I also wonder,
since I *think* I know what they're driving at, just how I would word
the claim to avoid ambiguity. On the other hand, probably they
don't *want* to avoid ambiguity.

There is an ad for a toothbrush that "cleans deep between each
tooth". What sort of imaginary space lies between a tooth? Another
one shows a rear view of a man who is cleaning his teeth while a
voice says: "This man is a dentist, which raises the question: 'What
brand of toothbrush does he use?'." Well, it *might* raise the question, but not necessarily. It certainly wouldn't spring to my mind,
and if it did, it would be pretty easy to predict that the answer
would not be one of the sponsor's competitors. At least they didn't
say "which begs the question".

I've dealt with "begging the question" elsewhere, but here's an
example of it from a commercial for a cleanser: "Vim can't scratch

because it's a liquid." It has not been established (and never will be) that liquids can't scratch. The statement is fallacious.

"Engineering demanded that only a five-cylinder engine would be right for this automobile, so we built it." So says a commercial for the Acura Vigor. Built what? The car? The engine? Does this mean anything at all?

Neo-Citran, a patent medicine said to alleviate symptoms of the common cold, boasts that "We've always been there". That seems to me to be patently false, but, since we all know that false advertising is against the law, I must be missing something. I have no idea what. I'm not sure, but I think I can remember a time when Neo-Citran was *not* there.

A commercial for a fast-food chain advertises a sandwich that comes with "a sauce you pour on yourself". That one, I am sure, was an absolutely deliberate attempt to say something people would talk about.

One of the most offensive TV advertising practices is signalled by the line, frequently heard in certain baseball telecasts, "This pitching change is brought to you by [say] Remington". In fact it is a team manager that brings you the pitching change, and Remington that is bringing you an opportunistic commercial. I don't mind it when a sponsor "brings" me the lineups or some group of statistics, but the idea of a sponsor bringing us a pitching change is simply stupid and insulting. The offence should not be blamed on the individual advertiser; it is a network practice, but the fact remains that the phrase is deliberately misused to convey a false impression. The line should be: "This unexpected opportunity to sneak in an extra commercial is being exploited by" whomever. I have seen a considerably smarter adaptation of this on CBS: "This relief break is sponsored by Rolaids." That's cute enough to be inoffensive.

This is from a big Ontario Hydro ad in *Time* magazine:

> With the Power Savers Plan, a qualified energy consultant
> visits the commercial, industrial or institutional facility of
> each participating business to audit its energy consump-
> tion...Ontario Hydro and local municipal utilities maintain
> an open line of communication with each participating
> business to assist them in implementing power saving mea-
> sures and to keep them informed about new programs and
> incentives as they become available.

Among other puzzlements, I fail to understand how each partici-
pating business was somehow transformed from an *it* to a *them*
between paragraphs of the same ad.

Ontario Hydro does a lot of advertising. That, too, baffles me. It
used to be that they were selling power, and wanted us to use more
of it, so the advertising made sense. Nowadays we are supposed to
be conserving power, so why the hell are they advertising?

I have seen innumerable real estate ads for houses with "a double-
car garage". I don't know anyone with a double car. Possibly the reference is to super-stretch limos, but the accompanying pictures
show garages that seem to be wider, not longer, than normal. Could
it be that they're talking about two-car garages? If so, why would
they not say that? Probably for the same reason they refer to a building lot as "pie-shaped" when they mean wedge-shaped. Most pies
are round; few building lots are.

Some such ads say the house provides an opportunity for "com-
muting with nature", which I take to mean that you can only get to
work via the scenic route.

There is something appealing about the real estate advertising
dodge of saying a property "has possibilities". This simply means it

needs a lot of work. The last time I was shopping for a home, one of my requests was to be shown nothing that had even so much as one possibility.

The following was in a newscast, not a commercial, but it seems to fit here. A blue-rinse matron was being interviewed in a TV person-on-the-street (POTS) survey on the takeover of the Simpsons department store chain by The Bay. Said she: "I've never shopped at The Bay. I've never been satisfied with what I've bought there." That line seems to be a cousin of the Tylenol commercials that have people saying "I'm not convinced Tylenol would work because I haven't tried it", and other strange things. I think another person says he hasn't tried Tylenol because he's not convinced it would work. I've lost my notes on that one, but, either way, it strikes me as inane. The commercials end with the endorser (now having tried the product) saying things like "It worked, it really worked. From now on, it's Tylenol for me". I'm quite sure that I haven't seen one in which the interviewee says "I haven't tried Tylenol because I'm afraid some nut has put cyanide in it". This surprises me, because these commercials contain such a convincing quality of spontaneity that you might think that could happen.

Commercials for painkillers generally give me a pain. There are far fewer over-the-counter generic anodynes than there are brand names. I would be more respectful of the advertising if the main ingredient of each brand were named, rather than being referred to as "the ingredient most doctors recommend" or some such.

The ones that tout "extra strength" are particularly irritating. These claims generally mean only that one tablet contains, say, half again as much acetylsalicylic acid (or acetophenetidin, or acetaminophen, or whatever) as another. The most commonly recommended dose of Aspirin is two tablets, but, in some circumstances, you may take three. If you want to rush out and buy the extra-strength package in order to achieve the same dosage with only two tablets, go ahead and be the sucker the ad writers are playing you for. They are counting on people being bewitched by the magic term *extra strength,* which actually means almost as little as "two scoops of raisins".

They also play games with such meaningless phrases as "contains two of the ingredients most recommended by doctors", not telling us what those ingredients are. It is quite obvious that they feel a lot more comfortable if we don't know exactly what their product contains.

In their relentless pursuit of gullible customers, advertisers often tell us that "similar" products are advertised nationally for significantly more money. The catch-word here is *similar,* which, contrary to what the hucksters hope you believe, does *not* mean identical, or anything like it.

One of the best and most enduring advertising slogans ever devised was RCA Victor's "The music you want when you want it". Terse, yet euphonious, it delivered its persuasive message effectively and grammatically, and, evidently, sold many phonograph records. When RCA introduced its videodisc players in the 1980s, therefore, one might reasonably have expected to see "The movies you want when you want them". But what did their advertising geniuses come up with? "Watch what you want when you want", that's what. It may be alliterative, but it is also solecistic, and thus is without charm. For various reasons, I didn't expect these machines to sell, and they didn't. I don't think that was because of the slogan but I'd like to think that the slogan didn't help.

Here's a piece of promotional copy:

> The Whig-Standard is one of Canada's only daily newspapers to produce its own Saturday magazine, which is filled with feature stories, in depth reporting, thoughtful essays, book reviews, puzzles, movie reviews, popular and classical music, and more. It's part of our special Saturday package, which also includes colored comics, TV Times, People in the Limelight, and other features on top of our regular daily news package.

What does "one of Canada's only daily newspapers" mean? Possibly *only* should have been *few*. Is the popular and classical music in the form of sheet music or recorded music? Either way, it's certainly an unusual bonus. Who stole the hyphen from *in-depth*? "On top of"? Surely they mean *plus* (which would have been fine here).

This is not really terrible, but when you consider that its purpose is to promote the sale of a newspaper that has at times produced some excellent writing, it is pretty bad. My point is simply that I would not feel encouraged to subscribe to any publication that advertises itself with that kind of prose.

Currently there is a lot of fuss being made by consumer groups and others about honesty and accuracy in labelling, but not much is being said about readability. I'll give you just one example.

A while back, the aphids had pretty much taken control of our garden. On someone's recommendation, I went out and bought a container of Fossil Flower natural bug killer for the roses. I read the label, as I had been brought up to do, and it said "Read label before using". Had I not been reading it already, I would have missed that, but, anyway, I took it to mean that I should read the rest of the directions on the label, and I did so, not without giggling at the implication that if one of your fish should happen to swallow some of the stuff you should induce vomiting and rush him to a hospital. The directions, however badly written, were understandable right down to "Repeat at frequent intervals".

If I had to do it all over again, I'd just giggle at that, too, and not bother wondering whether it meant every ten seconds or every ten years. But no, I had to start thinking about the fact that *frequent intervals* is a very common phrase, on labels and elsewhere, and wondering why that is so. The only reason I can think of for its popularity is that it doesn't really mean anything at all. *Interval* means, quite simply, a space or period of time between two things or events. *Frequent* is defined in lesser dictionaries (the *OED* gives it seven columns of type) as meaning, among other things, happening or occurring at short or brief intervals, so *frequent intervals* surely is redundant and should be replaced with *frequently*. But *frequently* doesn't really mean anything, either, unless it's modified in some way. You might say that you read labels more frequently than you used to, I suppose, but that still doesn't tell me anything unless I know how frequently you used to read them. I never did get to the bottom of all this. That happens to me frequently.

Anyway, the stuff got rid of the aphids and also furnished me with a good example of the frequent futility of label-reading. I won't even mention the line "Use only as directed".

Superchannel, the old pay-TV movie service, used to warn viewers that the upcoming movie was being presented "uncut and in its entirety", and prescribed the exercise of "viewer discretion". It was a long time before editorial discretion was exercised and someone there realized that it would be pretty hard to show a movie in its entirety if it had been cut.

More recently, the warning was that the film contained coarse language, or scenes of extreme violence, or nudity, or explicit sexuality, or all of the above, "which may be offensive to some viewers, and therefore the film is recommended for mature audiences only".

Did they really mean that? Did they want to say to me, a person who was paying them many dollars a month for their service, that if I found any of those things offensive, I was immature? I don't think they were stupid enough to *want* to insult me so grossly, but they did it.

Years ago I was present at a public hearing of the Canadian Radio-television and Telecommunications Commission whereat a number of spokeswomen (and, I think, some spokesmen) for the feminist movement had made a major presentation, the thrust of which was that most television commercials were offensive to women. At the very end of the long discussion, the late, great critic Northrop Frye, then a member of the commission, quietly asked the chief spokeswoman if she would agree that most television commercials are also offensive to men. She said yes, and he said thank you.

Leaving aside the sexist aspect, I suggest, while supporting the principle that advertising is a vital component of our economic system, that most TV advertising is an affront to human dignity. To get back within the scope of this book, I'll just say that I hope there is a special place in hell for the people in the advertising industry who have crassly perverted our language in the pursuit of profit with no concern for the damage they wreak on our main means of understanding each other.

CHAPTER 4

Righting Words

I want to talk about diction in this chapter. Sad to say, *diction* is one of those words whose meanings have been spread and diluted to the point that I feel obliged to explain what I mean by them before I start throwing them around. The primary meaning has to do with the choice of words to express ideas, and that is the sense in which I will be using it. Pronunciation is discussed elsewhere. Some dictionaries will tell you that *diction* is appropriate for both purposes, but I don't buy that.

And yes, I know that here and elsewhere in this book I have used *talk* and *say* and *speak* when I mean write. That's bad diction. Sue me.

There's a saying: "The Greeks had a word for it." I don't think there would be such a saying if the English had a word for everything, but we don't, and neither, for that matter, do the Greeks. No language has all the necessary words, so we all steal from each other. It amuses me that much of our English vocabulary was imposed on us by the Norman conquest. Evidently it wasn't enough, because we still steal from the French at the drop of a chapeau. Meanwhile, conservative academics in France are climbing the walls because of the pollution of their language by the likes of *le big mac*. When I started driving, a half-century ago, it was quite acceptable to pull into a Quebec gas station and say *"Fillez le tank and checkez les tires"*. It would be done. Possibly this is not the case today. Things have changed a bit there.

Several things can happen when things reach a point at which we need a word we don't have. One of the easiest solutions to the problem, and possibly the best, is to swipe one from another language. Another is to put one together from classical roots. A third, which is perhaps the most common, and certainly the worst, is to pervert an English word. There are others, but let's look at these three now.

For the first, one of the words the Greeks had was *kudos*, which means praise. It appears to have crept into English about 150 years ago as a part of university slang. Today we are faced with such abominations as the remark of a so-called film critic on CNN, who told us that *"Driving Miss Daisy* is worth every kudo it's collected"*. *Kudos* is not the plural of anything. There is no such thing as a "kudo". The *RH-II*, in one of its most galling entries, says there is, but I'm just not buying it. It's not the best illustration in this context, because I don't think there was any real need to import a synonym for *praise* except in the minds of some who wished to flaunt their erudition, but now we're stuck with it, and with its misuse by those who seem to want to flaunt their ignorance.

For the second, shortly after the turn of the century it became apparent that somewhere along the line someone was going to have to coin a word for the technology that would enable us to have a box in the livingroom that would show us pictures of something that was happening somewhere else. Someone came up with *television,* and it stuck, to the great distress of purists who were offended by the fact that *tele* (meaning from afar) came from Greek and *vision* (meaning see) came from Latin. I have heard *television* called a bastard word. Certainly it is the outcome of linguistic miscegenation.

But it has served us well enough. There were those who would have favoured *video* for the purpose, but if that had prevailed, what would we have done later on when we developed the word-need that is now served by *video,* which has come to mean a piece of recorded television?

Some people might be surprised that *television* was coined almost a half-century before the medium became a fact of life for all of us. They might be even more surprised to learn that, in a very real sense, television was invented before radio, but it was of no practical use *until* radio was invented. This is a digression I won't pursue, but it might amuse you to look into it.

For the third, we have long needed a word to describe people or actions that show contempt for standards of honesty or morality, especially when it comes to exploiting the scruples of others. We did not create or import a word for this purpose. Instead, we chose to corrupt an existing word. So, if I want to describe, say, certain television evangelists, I might call them cynical. However, the basic meaning of *cynical* is something else. A cynic is someone who is distrustful of any claim of selfless motivation on the part of others. The word comes from the name of a sect of philosophers in ancient Greece, the most famous of whom was Diogenes. A modern cynic is the guy who knows there's no such thing as a free lunch.

George Bernard Shaw wrote that "the power of accurate observation is commonly called cynicism by those who have not got it", which in itself is a rather cynical remark.

At any rate, *cynical* is now forced to do double duty, and that is an unfortunate thing to happen to any word. When I accuse the president of a large company of being cynical (new sense) in respect of his stance as a public-spirited corporate citizen, he might accuse me of being cynical (old sense), and anyone privy to this exchange might be pardoned for not knowing what in hell either of us was talking about.

Finally, here's a need that remains unfulfilled. We do not have adequate, widely accepted words for people who live together without going through the formality of marriage, although I do believe that there are quite a few of us. To use *husband* or *wife* suggests an unjustified claim to a certain legal status. *Spouse* is acceptable, but not precise enough, since it can be used for both unmarried and married people. The best attempt I've run into is *co-vivant(e)*, but it has not, as far as I know, achieved wide acceptance. My own entry is a pun: *comanditario,* which is Spanish for sleeping partner (in the business, not the bedroom, sense). No one I've ever tried it on has been in the least amused. Perhaps you can come up with something.

During live CBC coverage of one of the earlier constitutional conferences, Peter Mansbridge told us that the prime minister was now "gavelling the meeting to order". I was already reaching for a dictionary when I heard Mr. Trudeau say he was going to "inverse the usual order", and thought perhaps I had learned two new verbs in a matter of seconds. Not so. There is, of course, no such verb as *gavel.* It's a noun, and that's that. You call a meeting to order, with or without using a gavel as a means of attracting attention. (Furthermore, you do not normally pound a gavel; you pound *with* a gavel, although I suppose you *could* pound a gavel, perhaps with another gavel, if you happened to have two handy.)

However, no matter how wrong Trudeau may have been about many things, his use of *inverse* was absolutely correct, albeit a bit quaint. *Inverse* is, indeed, a transitive verb, although the *OED* qualifies it with a *now rare,* and it simply means invert. It has always been pleasant, and by no means impossible, to catch Mr. Trudeau committing a solecism or barbarism, but it pays to look before you leap.

It was a problem unique to such oral means of communication as broadcasting that brought about the destruction of *momentarily,* which for hundreds of years meant for a short time. A newspaper writer is not likely to be called upon to tell us that something is going to happen a moment from now; a broadcaster is. And so broadcasters, with characteristic indifference to good diction, began using *momentarily* for that purpose, so diligently that today those of us who wish to use the word correctly must, for fear of being misunderstood by a generation educated by television, resort to some unsatisfactory circumlocution.

While the verbal offences of journalistic dunderheads deserve unrelenting anger, at times it is difficult not to smile. A commentator told us (and it was no slip of the tongue or typewriter — he said it twice) that the provincial premiers were blaming the failure of the constitutional conference on the prime minister's "intransience". While it might be true that some premiers yearn for a more transient prime minister, the context should suggest to anyone, especially a professional communicator, that *intransigence* was meant.

The same culprit might plead that his faulty diction is "not very unique". Possibly he likes the sound of the word *unique,* and prefers it to *unusual,* which is one of several words he could have used to say what he meant. *Unique* has a unique meaning, and is in danger of being made worthless by being forced to keep company with such inapplicable adverbs as *very, more, most, somewhat,* and *rather.*

Quarterbacks are supposed to be the intellectual elite among football players. Perhaps it was the desire to sustain or perpetuate that concept that drove Bob Griese, when asked about his plans for his career, to reply: "I really haven't made a determination." Perhaps a lineman would have said "I haven't decided", but that would be unquarterbackly language. A final note from the *New York Times* columnist William Safire, who, writing on the subject of vogue words, says: "I remain of two minds about *ambivalent*."

It is often said by those who care about such things that one reason for their concern about the decline of English is that language, in addition to being an instrument of communication, is an instrument of thought. The person who cannot express himself clearly probably is incapable of thinking clearly. With that in mind, it is a truly terrifying experience to tune in the television coverage of the debates of the House of Commons.

I heard an Hon. Member speak of "a hypothetical assumption". What it was I do not know, because he had jolted me onto another tack. I was wondering what sort of assumptions he assumed existed, other than hypothetical ones. Also, I was hypothesizing that this was no harmless redundancy, no forgivable slip of the tongue. Indeed, I came to presume that it was an indication that he didn't know what he was talking about, and therefore was not worth listening to. So instead of listening, I gave some time to wondering what he would say if asked to explain the difference between *assume* and *presume*.

(A presumption is something you believe until or unless proven wrong; an assumption is an hypothesis. And it is neither incorrect nor pompous to use *an* before an unstressed syllable beginning with H, although Fowler says the practice is disappearing. He adds that you can't have it both ways: if you say *an*, don't aspirate the H. Hokay!)

The writer or speaker who forces us to pause and ask ourselves if he is, in fact, saying what he means is doing himself a disservice. That same day in the House, Herb Gray, the Liberal Cabinet minister then in charge of bailing out Chrysler, said: "The decision was made by myself." (The pompous or ignorant abuse of reflexive pronouns is widespread in government circles.) One could presume he meant "I made the decision". Perhaps he merely wished to use *myself* as an intensive: "I, myself, made the decision." Or maybe he meant that no one concurred in the decision. Or possibly he merely meant that, when he made it, he was alone in his office or bathroom or wherever he goes to decide things. Whatever he meant (even though there can't be much doubt about it), he didn't say it correctly.

Usage doesn't have to be "wrong" to be bad. One February, *The Globe and Mail* informed us that "most of Canada has been basking in above-freezing temperatures". I don't know about you, but, although I welcome the February thaw, I wasn't doing a hell of a lot of basking. You bask in warmth. Certainly, it could be argued that, in winter in many parts of this country, an above-freezing tempera-ture could be called relatively warm, and perhaps the writer should be forgiven a frivolous use of *bask*, if, indeed, the writer was being frivolous. It's a reflection on the condition of newspaper writing today that I don't feel secure in making that assumption. When a hostage was released by his terrorist captors and was described in the press as "basking in his new-found freedom", I think the writer was playing fast and loose with the word.

One of the buzzwords to gain favour in the late 1980s was *horizon*. It's a wonderful word; not mellifluous, perhaps, but rich in conno-tations of challenge and adventure and mystery and hope. It seemed a natural prey for those yahoos who sit around board-rooms perverting the language to contrive a jargon they think makes them sound important.

Now, instead of saying "We have three months to do this", they say "We have a three-month horizon on this project". This locution serves no purpose. It merely debases an irreplaceable word. Doubtless its users would attempt to justify themselves by saying it helps them to liaise with others who speak only jargon. I would not be surprised to hear one of them say "Let's horizon this for mid-August".

Buzzwords (a buzzword itself) no doubt will always be with us, and one might do well to look for a bright side to their existence. They are, in fact, neologisms, in one sense of that word. A neologism can be either a new word or a new meaning for an established word. There is some need for a new word to convey that second meaning of *neologism. Buzzword* almost does the job, but it is limited by a connotation of faddishness.

Some buzzwords survive their vogue and settle down as permanent residents in our vocabulary, simply because they fill a need. One such might be *prestigious.* One sees in the papers that more and more people are winning prestigious awards. Indeed, the reader might well wonder whether there is any other sort of award. Are there, perhaps, ignominious or degrading awards? There are, of course, booby prizes, but few of their recipients boast about them. Yet there are so many awards being dealt out these days that their winners (or their winners' press agents) feel the need of some qualifying term. It is no longer enough for the CBC, say, to announce that one of its programs has won an international award; it has to be a prestigious international award, or else it has to be awarded by, perhaps, a prestigious film festival.

It's not a happy choice. *Prestigious* used to denote trickery or deceit. (*Prestige,* meaning the power to command, or the state of commanding, admiration or esteem, came from the Latin for an illusion or a juggler's trick. In the last century it swung around to mean a blinding or dazzling influence, and then came to refer to the influence or reputation derived from past performance.) But there

was a real need for an adjective to describe something that is generally held in high regard, and *prestigious,* which was serving little
purpose with its established meaning, was conscripted for the job,
probably by people who did not know that meaning and simply
took it as an extension of *prestige.* However, the accepted meaning
of *prestigious* had not changed as quickly as had *prestige,* and still, to
some readers, it retains its suggestion of deceit, and perhaps it's fit-
ting that the word used to describe so many of these awards may
suggest that there is something illusory about the honour bestowed
on their recipients.

The word seems to have fallen into disuse during the first half of
this century. My favourite desk dictionary — which was published
in 1954, weighs ten pounds, three ounces, and defines *myrmeco-*
phagus — does not even mention *prestigious.* Since we weren't
making much use of the word during all those years, I suppose we
can't complain about the publicists' picking it up for their own purposes, but I think we all ought to regard with suspicion anything
that it's used to describe. I suggest that *lustrous* might serve the purpose better in many cases.

Buzzwords seem usually to emanate from places of high power,
high tension, high profile. They come from corporations, bureau-
cracies, advertising, the space program. One of the most fecund
sources in recent history was the Nixon White House-of-ill-repute,
and it is one of the later graduates of that institution, Alexander
Haig, who for some time was doing for the English language what
Attila the Hun did for European culture. Much has been written
about his contributions to bafflegab, but let's take a look at just one
of his barbarisms: "IMpact", which he uses as a verb. Now, *imPACT*
is an established verb, meaning to jam something against or into
something else. But *IMpact* is a noun, and has to do with two things
coming together violently, or colliding. Haig seems to use it as a

verb when he merely wants to say *affect*, or, perhaps, *affect seriously*, and he might earn more respect were he to simply say what he means.

He is not alone in this, of course. *Impact* has been on the endangered list for a long time. One time I wanted to demonstrate to someone that CNN is a generous source of solecisms, and switched it on to wait for the first one. Before the picture had stopped jiggling I was rewarded with this: "...the point at which the airplane impacted the ground". I do not like to be made to giggle while listening to a report of a tragic accident, but I had to react to the fact that this was, in an odd way, a correct use of *impact* as a verb. Undoubtedly, a falling airplane would impact the ground on which it fell, since the verb means pack down tightly. However, it does not mean hit, which I am certain was the word the speaker was searching for so desperately when he hit on *impact*.

A critic wrote: "Othello was the paragon of the jealous man." That sounds ridiculous, but it's a tough one to shoot down. Jealousy is a flaw; paragons are flawless. But if I say that *paragon* means model of perfection, the writer might say "That's what I mean: he's a perfect model of the jealous man". However, I say, no matter how you play around with words, that a perfect model is not a model of perfection (unless, perhaps, you're talking about Claudia Schiffer), and it was a wrong use of *paragon*. He might have said *epitome*. He still would have been wrong, but *epitome* is so widely used to mean what he was trying to say that I'd be willing to let it slide. Anyway, Othello sure was one jealous guy.

A reader once nailed me for a misuse of *convince* in a column. "It does not mean persuade", he wrote. I had written of wanting to convince someone to do something, when what I meant was that I wanted to persuade him to do it. Or, possibly, I meant that I wanted to convince him that it was the right thing to do. I don't remember. Although I remain neither convinced nor persuaded that there is no circumstance in which it would be permissible to substitute the one for the other, he was absolutely right in taking me to task. I was chagrined.

Incidentally, I grew up convinced that *chagrin* meant anger, and went on believing it until an angry editor persuaded me to look it up in a dictionary, which said "chagrin — what you are feeling at this moment". Obviously, this was the same dictionary used by Mr. Wilson in *Harvey*, and if you don't know what I mean by that, you missed a great play.

There are some largely ignored rules about the use of *over* in place of *more than*. I don't like it, but I'm sure we're stuck with it. I don't think anyone can be faulted for saying he's over forty, but I don't think I would say that I flew over over five countries on my vacation. I don't think it's terrible to say that the temperature is over eighty when it's more than eighty degrees above zero, but it would be a bit much to say the party was over over two hours ago. *More than* is correct, it doesn't sound stilted, and is almost as easily mouthed (especially when contracted, as it almost inevitably is, to *more'n*). Why not use it?

There is also the question of whether *more than one* is singular or plural. Theodore Bernstein explains that it's technically plural but takes a singular verb "by attraction" — that is, the verb is "attracted" to the *one* and to the singular noun that follows it. "Attraction" is a term used by grammarians when they feel obliged to condone a bit of usage that is patently wrong. But then they don't help matters much when they start talking about "acceptable attraction" and "unacceptable attraction" and the grey areas between the two. Some authorities go on at great length on "the proximity principle", but the *good* reason for not saying "this presents more than one problems" is that it sounds funny.

An *accolade,* properly, is an embrace or slap on the shoulder with the flat of a sword, signifying the conferral of knighthood. That's what it is, and, according to the *OED,* that's all it is (except to musicians and mathematicians in very special senses). It might, by reasonable extension, mean the bestowal of an honour. The permissive U.S. dictionaries now approve its misuse as an expression of praise, and that's going too far. But *fulsome* still means what it has meant for hundreds of years: disgustingly excessive. When the former prime minister Pierre Trudeau announced one of his resignations, many reporters were telling us that this or that person had given him an accolade, which I took to mean that, as I have always suspected, he must be the most be(k)nighted leader this country has ever had. When they reported that he had received this or that *fulsome accolade*, well, I didn't know what to think. These days, when a journalist uses *fulsome,* we are left to try to deduce from the context whether he means it or simply doesn't understand it. Usually it's safe to assume the latter.

A question I dread hearing is "Which is correct?". It usually means there is tough sledding ahead.

A common example is "Which is correct, *compared with* or *compared to*?". The questioner obviously is seeking a simple answer and is unlikely to pay attention to, let alone remember, the proper reply.

It is, of course, not a question of right and wrong, but one of distinction. It is not terribly difficult. Use *to* only if you wish to suggest or state a similarity. If you compare Smith's writing *to* Hemingway's, you are saying that Smith is in the same class as Hemingway. But if you compare it *with* Hemingway's, you are making a detailed examination of the similarities and differences between them. You might then decide that, compared *with* Hemingway, Smith falls short.

It should be obvious that you can't compare Hemingway either with or to Smith's writing, or vice versa: "Compared with Hemingway, Smith's writing is abominable", but that is a terribly common error, not only with *compare*, but with *like*, as in "Like many of us, his vices included smoking". Beware comparing things that are not comparable. You might, however, like to think a bit about whether one incomparable thing might be compared to another. I'll leave that with you.

Compare does provide some right-or-wrong answers for those who like them. As an intransitive verb, it always requires *with*. To say that a girl's looks "cannot compare to" those of her sister is wrong. "In comparison to" is *never* right, although you could say that you, too, had made a comparison of Smith with Hemingway and decided that any comparison of Smith to Hemingway was invalid.

The cliché about "comparing apples *and* oranges" is wrong. You could compare apples and oranges to tree-borne fruits, or you could compare them with bedroom slippers, but *compare* must have either *with* or *to*; *and* simply will not do.

Someone wrote me to say that I was wasting time fretting over *compared with* and *compared to*. "A simple syntactic rule suffices", he said. "There are exact synonyms for the two most common meanings of *compare*, viz. *contrast* and *liken*. Substitution of either suggests the correct proposition [*sic*], as in *contrasted with* and *likened to*." I do not prepose [*sic*] to do much more fretting about the matter, and I think that this is more a question of diction than of syntax, but I appreciate the facility of his suggestion and pass it along for your consideration. *Likened to* I like, but I suspect that as many people would choose the wrong preposition with *contrasted* as do with *compared.*

I don't think *astronaut* is a very good word. The connotation of navigating through the stars is a bit grandiose. The Russians' coinage of *cosmonaut* is a bit more down-to-earth. *Astronautics* was with us before the U.S. space program was conceived, and *Webster* defined it as the science dealing with the possibility of travelling through interplanetary space. I'd have thought *interstellar* would be etymologically more appropriate than *interplanetary.* Applying *astronauts* to the crew of a U.S. space shuttle, which does not go beyond a low-level orbit around Earth, is really pushing it. I was pleased to hear a CNN reporter calling them *shuttlenauts.* That's an ugly coinage, but is suitably less pretentious than the others. However, I had to draw the line when the Biosphere II project got under way in 1991 and CNN wasted no time in dubbing its occupants *bionauts,* which is simply stupid.

I've been poring over the *OED* (not pouring over it, as the younger journalists do) in search of some justification of the common use these days by sports writers of *settle for.* I couldn't find *settle* with *for* at all before my vision began to blur, although the dictionary deals with thirty-six broad senses of the verb. However, for the purpose of this argument, let's say that to settle for something is to reach a compromise: you owe me ten dollars but can only pay me five; all right, I'll settle for that. It's better than nothing.

That seems to me to be acceptable idiomatic use. But I don't know what to make of the sports writer who says that the Blue Jays took an early 3-1 lead, but after so-and-so doubled with two on in the ninth they had to *settle* for a tie, or that the favourite in a horse race *settled* for third place. I don't know what that means. If *settle* means anything in this use, it means agree to accept something less than what was sought. If a baseball team settles for a tie, it implies that a choice was made, and that must mean that the game was fixed. And if a horse settles for third place, surely that gives new meaning to the term *horse sense.*

No. This is egregious misuse of *settle.* However, who cares. The sports pages contain some of the worst writing in the paper for the same reason (permissiveness) that explains why they also contain some of the best, and if we have to put up with a lot of stupid writing in order to encourage the development of some fine writing, well, maybe we should settle for that.

In the book *Megatrends,* John Naisbitt tells us cheerfully that we are rapidly changing from a manufacturing society to an information society. That was unquestionably the most frightening prediction of its year. Certainly we have the technology to make the transition in the next couple of decades.

But will we have the words?

CHAPTER 5

Sloppy Writing

Sloppy writing may stem from carelessness or ignorance or both. When I write (for publication) sloppily, I usually choose to attribute it to ignorance. I do care, but I don't know everything. (Of course, in news writing, deadline pressures often account for seeming carelessness, but they are too often used — by me, among others — as a convenient excuse.) Herein is a selection of examples of sloppy writing. I don't much care which of the above causes engendered them. Some of them seem to me to require no comment or explanation. I hope I am right about that.

It is common for reporters to tell us that a defendant "faces" a sentence of ten years and a fine of $50,000 if convicted, without mentioning that those are the maximum penalties, and that the person might get off with a mere slap on the wrist. It is seriously misleading to suggest that the maximum penalty is inevitable.

"A coroner's jury recommended that all alcoholic beverages *contain* a warning label." I think it would be sufficient to have it on the outside of the bottle. I don't know what could be done in bars.

A member of the federal Parliament: "Violence against women should be a priority of the government."

Global-TV News: "The hostages are thrilled to be home, as are their families."

A report on the buildup of coalition troops in Saudi Arabia: "That number could soon grow to 430,000 by next month."

The space shuttle "landed early to avoid forecasts of bad weather".

"Were it not for a daring rescue the life of a child may have been lost." (*May* and *might* are discussed elsewhere, but *might* was required here.)

An educational program informed us that warthogs' warts were "designed to" protect their eyes from the tusks of fellow warthogs. I suppose that creationists would have no problem with this one, but I have to wonder who did the designing.

A CBC report said "the government is trying to rush through legislation" to end a postal workers' strike. I believe that the government was trying to rush it through, not rush through it. A CBC interviewer asked a doctor charged in the wake of the Dubin report on the use of drugs by Canadian amateur athletes: "Do you regret any of the actions you're accused of performing?" A CBC reporter described "one of the many indignations suffered by the hostages".

Reporters have started referring to "charges of bribery" when they mean charges of accepting bribes. Surely that is no trivial distinction. Consider these: "The courts should be the sole judge of whether the accused is guilty of the crimes he committed." "Much will depend on the testimony of the woman he is accused of allegedly imprisoning."

Most people, it seems, talk of "falling between the cracks" instead of falling into them.

A reporter reported that the visiting team "denied the Blue Jays from scoring".

During the Gulf War, we were frequently told of missiles that were "launched at" Israel or Saudi Arabia. What was meant was that they were aimed at these targets. They were, of course, launched *at* (or *in* or *from*) some site in Iraq.

Many journalists apparently need to be told that an "aboriginal murder" is not the same as the murder of an aboriginal person.

"An agreement was reached after an 18-hour all-night bargaining session." One might assume that the session was held in the far north, but in fact it was in Toronto, where the nights sometimes seem that long but never are.

About the breaking up of families in wartime, a reporter wrote that "an estimated ten million people were split up". What an image of carnage that evokes!

The slogan "A mind is a terrible thing to waste" seems to make its point, but it is nevertheless sloppy writing. I don't know why it couldn't be "It's a terrible thing to waste a mind".

Here is the opening paragraph of a news story published by *The Toronto Sun*: "One of two men who escaped with his life as O'Neil (Dave) Keane died in an ambush-style shooting successfully appealed a life sentence for the murder of a woman almost four years ago." This may be the worst lead I have ever read. I pass it along to provide an opportunity for people in less populous centres to see an example of the sort of clear and precise writing that is available to big-city newspaper readers.

I didn't even wince when a TV news reporter informed me that "a police guard was posted so as not to disturb the evidence". Somewhere in the dank dungeons of my mind, a tiny slave wearing a headset translated the line for me, and we moved on to the next item. But, for some reason, the original version stayed on to haunt me. Suppose the translator had been on a coffee break. I guess I would have thought the reporter was suggesting that it was clever of the police to avoid posting the guard in a manner that *would* disturb the evidence. (I also wondered why the reporter thought it was even worth mentioning that police investigating a murder did not wish the evidence to be disturbed.)

This was a minor gaffe. Probably there were a dozen like it in the same newscast. They are so common that those few of us who are even aware of them tend to shrug them off. Certainly some slips are inevitable in that medium, since the reporter in some circumstances is under pressure and there is no opportunity for a copy editor to make corrections. But there ought to be a lot of wrist-slapping going on behind the scenes, and I doubt that there is any at all. It is worse when these things happen in newspapers, worse still when they happen in magazines, worse even than *that* when they happen in books. And when they happen in *text*books...

A news item about a new safety device for airplanes informed us in passing that "fires result in many crashes", an unfortunate choice of phrase that forced me to stop dead and try to figure out just what I was being told. Given that a fire may cause an airplane to crash or a crash may cause it to catch fire, the phrase could not be understood without a careful examination of the whole carelessly written item.

It had to be understood that the device was a powerful, smoke-penetrating emergency light, to be installed in the passenger cabin in order to alleviate blind panic and show the way to emergency exits once the aircraft was on the ground or water. It was not a device to aid the crew in fighting a fire that might cause a crash, but rather one designed to help passengers survive a fire that had been caused by a crash. It turned out that we were dealing with fires caused by crashes, rather than crashes caused by fires.

Why, then, was the writer telling us, as he unquestionably was, that fires cause many crashes? That might be true, but is not relevant here. Could it have been that he meant to say that fires result *from* many crashes? But that would hint, at least, that it is only when there are many crashes that we need fear fire. No, what he probably *thought* he was saying was that many crashes result in fires, and what he *should* have said was "many crashes result in fire". That probably would have escaped comment, although, in fact, it is not quite correct usage. When *result* is used with *from,* it means arise as a consequence of. When it is used with *in,* it means end or conclude as specified. Thus, while it is right to say that a fire resulted from a crash, it is wrong to say that the crash resulted in a fire, because the fire would have been only one effect of the cause, whereas *result* implies a totality of effects.

Probably I am now putting too fine a point on it. I would not be terribly upset by someone saying that a fire was *a* result of a crash, although I would balk at *the* result. And I would prefer to say the fire was a consequence rather than a result, or that the crash caused a fire, and reserve *result* for such uses as, for example, describing the relationship between careful planning and a successful operation.

A badly expressed statement need not be truly confusing to be a stumbling-block. A writer in *Saturday Night* magazine referred to a "serious disaster", causing at least one reader to pause and try to think (in vain) of an example of a disaster that should not be regarded as serious, and it's worth trying to avoid little disruptions that distract the reader. (That writer, by the way, is one of the best around. Nobody's perfect.)

A program description in a leading TV listings magazine told of a movie about a man who was appointed "to head up a vigilante group to rid greed and corruption from the community". I used to write about television regularly, and accurate program information is still important to me. Can I expect to get it from someone who writes like that?

A dispatch from Reuters, as printed in *The Globe and Mail*: "British novelist Penelope Lively was named the unexpected winner yesterday of Britain's top literary award, the Booker Prize." Is there a category for unexpected winners? Who was named the expected winner?

Having been driven nigh unto distraction by pitchmen offering me things "for free", I was pleased to read a piece of promotional material for a magazine that promised me, among other things, information on "how to rent the most popular videocassettes free". It was not, however, the absence of the offensive *for* that made me receptive to the offer, but the desire to have it explained to me how one could possibly rent *anything* free.

Politicians are perhaps fonder than anyone of spouting such lines as "the situation is unlikely to change in the foreseeable future". If they can foresee the future, they shouldn't say *unlikely*, because they would know for sure whether the situation is or is not going to change. The phrase also appears with astonishing frequency in the daily press, as it should, because if anyone actually can foresee the future, that's news. And you'll notice the phrase is always used in a negative sense: "not in the foreseeable future". They don't tell us what is going to happen. The term belongs in the astrology column, not the news pages.

We are incessantly being told that something is "three times faster" than something else, or that this contains "five times more" something than that. It should be three times *as fast,* or five times *as much.* Think about *twice,* which means two times. Nobody says "twice faster" or "twice more than", but I suppose someone will. I have heard "twice as many than" for "twice as many as".

Reading the daily papers, one of the most common errors to catch my eye is the unattached participle. Trying to figure out why this is so, writers seem to have no good reason for committing the error so often. Bewildering in its frequency, you can seldom get through a single page of a newspaper without stumbling over at least one example of it.

If reading the preceding paragraph didn't make you throw up, you need to read the following one.

There are many names for such offences. I am going to call them misdirected modifiers. The most egregious common example is the epidemic misuse of *hopefully* (which is dealt with at some length in the next chapter). But I can understand that misuse. There are many adverbs that can be used properly to modify a following sentence or clause rather than its verb only. Understandably, it is difficult to convince many people that *hopefully* is not one of them. But I cannot understand why a writer would write: "Walking across an icy street, a car skidded into him." (I found that sentence in a news story I was editing years ago. I returned it to the reporter, who "corrected" it by inserting *while* before *walking*. He's still in the business, though, and probably still trying to make cars walk.)

The misdirected modifier does not always lead to such obvious absurdities. The sentence "Leafing through the magazine, a colourful ad caught my eye" would certainly catch the eye of any thoughtful reader. "Leafing through the magazine, my eye was caught by a colourful ad" is no less incorrect, but it is less jarring and might pass unnoticed. Some of these errors are even condoned by authorities (including Fowler) who say usage has given the words the qualities of prepositions or adverbs, enabling them to stand alone without being hooked to a noun or pronoun. Fowler considers *considering* to be one such. He says we can say "Considering the circumstances, you were justified".

Considering the possibilities of misunderstanding, I say he's living dangerously. Consider this sentence: "Considering the odds, he made a wise bet." Who is considering the odds here? Am I telling you that I am considering the odds and then passing judgment on the wisdom of his bet, or am I telling you that he, after considering the odds, bet wisely? Sorry, I think that participle needs attaching.

Here's another one: "Speaking candidly, he's rude." What I

might mean is that when he speaks candidly, he's rude (but he's charming when he dissembles). Or perhaps I mean "Speaking candidly, I say he's rude", and if that's what I mean, that's what I should say.

Possibly the reason we are presented with so many misdirected modifiers is that the ambiguities they create are more often simply absurd than truly confusing. We are all too familiar with the likes of this: "A patient in General Hospital, his leg is broken in three places." That doesn't confuse us, since we *know* he was the patient, not his leg. Now try this one: "A patient in General Hospital, his mother spent the night at his bedside." Is it possible his mother was a patient there?

From a news report about a prisoner who had been freed on bail only to be arrested on another charge the following day: "After one day of freedom, a provincial judge denied bail." There you go — give a judge a little freedom and he'll turn nasty every time.

Here's one that delighted me recently: "A native of Calgary, his wife was born in Edmonton." We can laugh that off; we know what the writer meant. But suppose he writes this: "A Canadian, his wife was born in France." We can see that the writer is sloppy. What is he trying to tell us? His subject is a Canadian married to a French-woman? Or is his subject's wife a French-born, naturalized Canadian citizen? Suddenly he can no longer answer our criticism with that standard cop-out of the careless writer — "Oh, well, you know what I mean." We don't know. If this were a story about, say, a contested decision by the immigration department, the modifier might make the whole story incomprehensible to us.

I began by saying that I find it difficult to find reasons for the prevalence of this sin. Perhaps there is a clue in the fact that it is seldom committed in everyday speech. The constructions of such speech do not invite it. It is frequently committed by reasonably well-educated and articulate people who are not accustomed to writing. When they are required to write, they feel obliged to use constructions they believe are appropriate to formal writing.

That would explain the profusion of misdirected modifiers in the work of neophyte newspapermen and autobiographers, but these are errors that are so obvious and so easily avoided or corrected that there seems to be no rational explanation of the extent to which they litter the published work of paid writers.

I would like to direct the attention of every writer and editor in the English-speaking world to the middle of page 13 in *The Elements of Style*, where it is printed in large, bold, italic type: "A participial phrase at the beginning of a sentence must refer to the grammatical subject." There follows almost a full page of explanation and examples that should not be beyond the comprehension of at least some of the professional communicators who tirelessly flaunt their ineptitude by flouting this simple and sensible principle.

Having said all that, you will have to excuse me for yielding to the temptation to get in just one more of my own.

We were told that a General Motors layoff was suspected of being "in retaliation for the union's refusal to accept wage concessions". Perhaps the union refused to accept a proposal that it *make* concessions. It is, of course, possible to refuse to accept a concession, but it required an examination of the context in this case to understand that the writer was not saying what he meant.

The common expression *near miss* is much used (or misused) in the news media these days. There are sometimes news stories about two airplanes that almost collided. Some newspapers would call this a near collision; others would call it a near miss. I don't care for either of those expressions, and I would suggest, to keep things simple, that everyone shun such uses of *near*. Although Fowler says a near miss is a miss that is almost a hit, I don't think I could quickly distinguish between a near miss and a near hit the way the phrases are commonly used. To me, *near miss* connotes the proximity of an unattached young woman. A *near collision* is a collision that happens outside my house, which is on a busy street. Inserting a hyphen after *near* in such contexts only increases the confusion. Like so many journalistic attempts at terseness, this use is counterproductive. How about "a narrowly averted collision" or "two airplanes almost collided", or some such?

I am reasonably tolerant of sins committed by reporters working under deadline pressure, but I couldn't tolerate the following sentence from a front-page story in *The Globe and Mail* back when the New Democratic Party leader Ed Broadbent and the Liberal Cabinet minister Marc Lalonde were in a House of Commons that appears to me to have grown ever less gracious: "Mr. Broadbent had to ask his question instead of Mr. Lalonde." The trouble is not only that it's a terrible sentence and one that forces the reader to grope for its intended meaning but also that it spoiled the point of the quite amusing digression the writer was indulging in. An alert editor, by moving *instead* to the end of the sentence, could have saved the joke. Even simply wrapping *instead* in commas would have helped.

For some reason, a lot of funny statements come from hospitals. I've always enjoyed the sort of headline that reads "Shot three times by robber, policeman critical", to which the only possible answer is "Well, wouldn't you be?".

On a TV newscast, during a union's dispute with a hospital, a striking (in more ways than one) nurse told a reporter that "the critically ill will not suffer". That certainly beats Aspirin, I guess, but what about the aches and pains of those with lesser ailments?

That same week, a news story on a doctors' strike in Toronto read: "A hospital spokesman said the doctors' walkout will not have much effect on operations." I wonder who was performing the operations in the absence of the surgeons. A team of highly skilled spokesmen, perhaps. Surely one could expect someone who is paid to speak for hospitals to be a little more careful about the way he flings around such ambiguous words as *operations*.

A CBC musicologist (that's the FM equivalent of a disc jockey) was talking about a jazz musician who was given to "indulging in such excessive behaviour as dressing sartorially". Now, if dressing sartorially means anything at all, it means wearing clothes. If that, in the musicological world, is regarded as excessive behaviour, I think I'll go back to AM.

I loved the line spoken by a TV network newsperson who was reporting live from some scene of action and was having difficulty answering questions being put to her by her anchorman. Her explanation: "I can't see anything from this vantage point." While a vantage point doesn't by definition have to be a good one, the idea of a vantage point from which *nothing* can be seen tickled me.

A newspaper literary supplement reported that a best-seller had been translated into ten "different languages".

Comedian Jerry Lewis was appearing on Phil Donahue's TV talk show to promote a charity. He admitted that there were other charities that were "equally as important". "Equally as important", echoed his host.

A senior TV newsman told us of an accident in which "a passenger was shook up".

A newspaper critic, earnestly attempting to praise a performance, called it "stultifying".

We're in trouble. We learn by example, and these are examples of the examples we learn by. Donahue, I'm sure, would say "equally important" or "as important", but he slavishly repeated Lewis's mistake, thereby reinforcing it.

The TV newsman, I'm sure, grew up listening to Elvis Presley singing about being "all shook up".

Stultify is not a word in everyday use. The recommended procedure when one encounters such a word is to look it up in a dictionary, but most readers don't. Instead of discovering that it means cause to appear foolish or worthless, many will simply adopt it as a term of praise and spread the error. I have no idea what the critic thought he meant, but I do know that such misuse stultifies critics.

There was a fuss in our neighbourhood about a proposed rezoning bylaw. Some concerned residents persuaded our alderman to oppose it. In a letter riddled with solecisms, the alderman reported to her constituents that "I moved to have the By-law rescinded. It was carried unanimously by City Council".

I tripped first on her use of *rescinded*. You can't rescind a law that isn't a law yet. But what was important was that she was reporting that the cause was lost. The only noun in the first sentence was *By-law* (which needs neither a capital letter nor a hyphen), so that was the only possible antecedent for the *It* that began the second sentence. Council had passed a law, but it appeared she had moved to have it rescinded before it was passed. Maybe. Anyway, it seemed that the controversial building would be built. A day or so later, I took another look at the letter and started wondering how the bylaw could have been passed "unanimously" when she was opposed to it. To this day, I really don't know what she was talking about.

Wouldn't it be grand if the alderman's old English teacher had received that letter, believed what it said, and rushed out and sold his house below market value?

A writer for *The Globe and Mail* reported that a building on a movie set is "an almost exact replica" of another. A replica, the *OED* tells us, is "a copy, duplicate, or reproduction of a work of art; properly, one made by the original artist". This was not a replica, then. Had it been, it would have been as like the original as possible, so "almost exact" is redundant. The writer probably meant it was a good copy.

Comprise is a word used by many people. Not too many of them know what it means, although many think they do. Some authorities suggest avoiding *comprise* and using *include* instead, but there is a valid distinction: the whole comprises all the parts, but may include some or all of them. Your diningroom suite, perhaps, includes a table and a sideboard, but it comprises a table, a sideboard, eight chairs, and a thingummy. *Comprise* can be a useful word, but is not for people who eat in the kitchen.

"He will appear in court today to set a date for a preliminary hearing." Or so reporters frequently report. But *he* doesn't set the date. The judge does.

A wire-service story said "The court found the company's emergency system completely lacking". I simply do not know what that means, and the context was of no help. Without *completely*, I'd have assumed that the system was deficient or incomplete. Could it have been completely incomplete? Did the writer mean that the court found that there was no system? If so, why did he not say that? Was he about to say it was completely lacking in some specific thing when he was cut short by some emergency that the system lacked the capability to cope with? I guess I'll never know.

Our one-time (one *short* time) prime minister of Canada and long-time external affairs minister, Joe Clark, once read a major statement in the Commons in which he spoke of "reducing the danger of nuclear conflict". If we do have a nuclear war, I don't think anybody, even the mighty Joe Clark, can do anything to make it less dangerous. If he was talking about the threat, or the probability, or the possibility of nuclear war, he should have used one of those words. I repeat, this was a prepared statement (probably written by a committee) of considerable importance, not an off-the-cuff speech.

In the years since the beginning of live television coverage of the debates of the House of Commons, I have become accustomed (but not inured) to the grotesque maltreatment of the English language (to varying degrees) by all of our elected representatives, and I often wonder what is to become of us if there is not one person in that chamber who can be relied on to say precisely what he (or she) means.

But Mr. Clark was our nation's top diplomat. I was brought up to believe that diplomats were required to be very careful about their diction, since one carelessly chosen word could start a war. That was one reason that French, honoured for its subtlety and respected for the consistency imposed on it by the French Academy, was until recently the language of diplomacy. (Did it make you giggle or scare the hell out of you to imagine Joe Clark going all over the world negotiating our future in *his* French?)

Perhaps this comes down to a question of semantics, rather than diction. Doubtless Mr. Clark and his aides and writers could cite dictionaries that would support his use of *danger* in that sense. I had a writer friend who had, as do I, a large number of dictionaries. Whenever I challenged him on what I considered to be his misuse of a word, he always was able to find at least one authority to back him up. When once I chided him for defining *emergent* in the sense of pressing, he had no trouble finding a popular modern dictionary that supported him. Indeed, the *OED* cites, but does not condone, examples of that use as early as 1706, but I suggest that the only thing that that indicates is that the misuse of words is by no means peculiar to modern times. If one wishes to say *urgent,* that is what one should say. *Emergent* means rising out of a surrounding medium, and any figurative use of it should be based on the literal sense. There might have been an emergent danger of nuclear war breaking out in the wake of the loss of central control of the Soviet Union in the summer of 1991. That was considered by many to be a matter for urgent concern, but that still doesn't make *emergent* mean urgent. There exists, of course, danger that someone might start a nuclear war, and that, presumably, is the danger that Mr. Clark wanted reduced. But that is not what he said.

I am now prepared to be scoffed at by people who will tell me that it's perfectly obvious what was meant. I'm used to that, but the attitude of those who dismiss fine distinctions as inconsequential quibbles creates an environment that encourages dangerous misunderstandings.

Here is a sentence from a *Globe and Mail* news story: "The report was immediately dismissed as a 'complete fabrication' by Mr. Mulroney's press secretary, William Fox." Is it perfectly obvious what was meant there? No. The writer might claim that it is, but even a careful examination of the context does not rule out the possibility that the reporter was quoting some anonymous person who had called Mr. Fox a liar.

This is a useful example of the pitfalls of the passive, a voice much favoured by journalists trained to put first things first. In this example, the fact that the report was dismissed was more important than the identity of the dismisser. The passive construction enabled the reporter to report in the descending order of importance, but it also resulted in ambiguity. And ambiguity can lead to lawsuits.

Or even wars.

CHAPTER 6

Lost Causes

I had planned to discuss, in this chapter, various vile trends that seem to me to be beyond any hope of reversal, but I have found it difficult to decide what belongs here. It is, of course, a matter of subjective judgment, and so depends on the mood I'm in. Sometimes I think the whole book should be in under this heading; the next day I might think (hopefully) that some miracle will take place and all the English-speaking peoples of the world will unite in an effort to save the language. There are many misuses that I think, even on my most cheerful days, have gone beyond the point of no return, and I'll (hopelessly) deal with a few of them here.

One of the signs I look for in deciding what is a lost cause is the abandoning of a distinction by some of the people I have relied on to hold the line. The eminent political columnist William Safire, who, on the side, writes the "On Language" columns in *The New York Times,* is probably the most popular and entertaining North American writer on the subject of English usage today. For all my admiration of him, I think he did us all a disservice by capitulating prematurely to the prevalent misuse of *hopefully.*

Some years ago, in reviewing Kingsley Amis's book *On Drink,* a witty compendium of advice to boozers, I felt unable to give unqualified approval to the work of anyone who would put ketchup in a Bloody Mary. Faced with a copy of Safire's *On Language*, the first of many enjoyable collections of his language columns, I felt unable to give unqualified approval to the work of anyone who approves the current misuse of *hopefully* for "I hope that" or "one hopes that" or "it is to be hoped that".

Safire offers a lengthy (and, I suggest, specious) argument in favour of acceptance of this barbarism. Essentially, he favours it "because no other word better substitutes for the awkward 'it is to be hoped that'".

That's silly. *Hopefully* has a useful, established meaning that should not be destroyed by misuse. Must we now search in a hopeful manner instead of searching hopefully? If we hope that a problem will be solved, Safire would have us say "Hopefully, the problem will be solved". If we have no hope of a solution, would he have us say "Hopelessly, the problem will be solved"? I think not.

The first person who had to refer to the offspring of a male ass and a female horse did not say "Well, since there's no such word as *mule*, I'll call it a rhinoceros". He invented a word, rather than messing up an existing one. (Our *mule* comes from the Latin *mulus*; nobody seems to know where *mulus* came from, but it means mule, which is about all I learned from an unusually frustrating excursion through a number of dictionaries.)

Interestingly, Safire says that if there were such a word as "hopably", it would do for *hopefully* what *regrettably* does for *regretfully*. Regretfully, he notes that there is, regrettably, no such word as "hopably", "so it makes no sense to keep fighting the extended use of 'hopefully'". What he evidently did not know is that the English language contains *hopeable*, which means "that may be hoped for". The *OED* calls it "rare", but if there is a great need for such a word, surely it would be better to revive *hopeable*, and give it an adverbial form, than to debase *hopefully*.

Still, "hopeably" would have to be understood to mean "it may be hoped that", rather than "it is hoped that" or "it is to be hoped that", and a further extension of meaning would be required to make it useful as an alternative to the misuse of *hopefully*. Perhaps Safire is right in saying that *hopefully* in its new sense has won the usage battle. Hopeably he is wrong. I hope so.

Safire is a modest man who does not try to pose as an authority. He offers opinions and arguments, and they merit respect. He is a professional writer, and a damn' fine one, enjoying an opportunity given to few professionals. A surgeon cannot cut about cutting; a cabbie cannot drive about driving. Arguably, a lawyer could argue about arguing, or an illustrator could illustrate the job of illustrating. Unquestionably, a writer can write about writing, and Safire does so in an entertaining and stimulating way. He has avoided (with difficulty, he confesses) the pitfall that threatens every writer who writes about writing: letting the fear of error stifle his style, and consequently writing pedantically in the hope of avoiding the inevitable niggling criticism of pedants.

He insists on his right to break both new ground and old rules, but, save for such exceptions as the one discussed above, he exercises it in an orderly and reasonable manner and only in the interest of improving the tools of his trade. His errors (or what he cordially invites us to perceive as errors) are to be rebuked gently, not reprimanded (look up that distinction), because he is a writer who cares about his craft. Would that there were more like him.

But...

Hopefully, as it is misused today, is a cop-out word. People who say something like "Hopefully, this crisis will be resolved peacefully" should be saying "I hope this crisis will be resolved peacefully", but for some reason they seem to be reluctant to admit to doing the hoping. If this is the case, they might be pardoned for saying "It is to be hoped that...". This gets them off the hook, since they are not coming right out and confessing that it is they who are hopeful. It doesn't matter that it is meaningless, since it serves this strange purpose without destroying the real value of *hopefully*, which might be used properly in something like "Hopefully, I kept watching television for news that the crisis had been resolved peacefully". (Or should that be *peaceably*? Actually, either will serve here, although there is a distinction.)

There are some tough arguments for condoning the misuse, or at least for tolerating it. One is that there seems to be a need for it, and we don't have a word that fills that need. Were "hopeably" to be commonly recognized, perhaps none of this would have happened. Regrettably, that is not the case. Fortunately, there is such a word as *regrettably*, which enables us to pounce on those who say something like "Regretfully, there is no hope". Happily, there are far fewer people who would do that than there are who would use *happily* when they mean *fortunately*.

The *RH-II* politely acknowledges that there are those who object strongly to the use of *hopefully* as a sentence modifier in the sense we are talking about, but says it has been used this way since the 1930s, and is "fully standard in all varieties of speech and writing". It goes on to say that "this use of *hopefully* is parallel to that of *certainly, curiously, frankly, regrettably,* and other sentence modifiers".

I can't quite buy that. Certainly, there is room for argument. Curiously, even lexicographers refuse to recognize that *hopefully* means full of hope, while *regrettably* does not mean full of regret. Frankly, though, I don't think there is any point in going on about *hopefully*. The misuse is well established. Oddly, although I still wince when I hear it, I have, God help me, found myself saying it.

Perhaps there is some point in going on about other sentence modifiers. *Thankfully* seems doomed to the same fate as *hopefully*, leaving us with the same questions: when a reporter says "Thankfully, no one was injured", who is it that is giving thanks? If it is the reporter, is it proper to inject this personal note? How long will it be before the same reporter says "Gratefully, welfare payments are being increased"? How about *personally,* which now should be placed on the endangered word list? Is it falling prey to the same infatuation with ellipsis that has damaged some of the words above? Such a statement as "Personally, I think the prime minister is an idiot" is common enough, and there's nothing really wrong with it. It could convey its message without *personally,* but, like the reflexive pronoun ("I, *myself,* think..."), the word emphasizes that this is being offered as one person's opinion. However, what is happening is that people are dropping the *I think* and writing "Personally, the prime minister is an idiot". That is still a statement, and I would assume that the writer still intended the use of *personally* to indicate that this was his own opinion, but it doesn't. It now means that the prime minister, as a person (and not necessarily as a prime minister), is an idiot.

That is pretty much what happened to *frankly,* also. The idea of using as few words as possible has long been drummed into young writers, who tend to overreact. The result is excessive ellipsis that leads to confusion. After all, *I think,* or some such phrase, doesn't take all that much space.

Further confusion is engendered by the fact that the *-ful* suffix doesn't always mean what it should. For example, while *hopeful* means full of hope, *hateful* does not (as might reasonably be expected) usually mean full of hate, but rather arousing or deserving hate — or, in short, *hateable. Hateable,* like *hopeable,* has been with us for centuries, but is largely ignored. *Webster* lists the variant *hatable* and simply says it means *hateable.* But, unlike many others, it does not list *hateable.* Even the best lexicographers occasionally nod.

I don't expect any resurgence of interest in the *shall/will* distinction. It is infrequently observed in modern North American writing. It isn't all that complicated, but it's perverse in its rule, and doubtless doomed by its own clumsiness.

The rule is that the future tense requires *shall* in the first person and *will* in the second and third, to express expectation or inevitability. To express determination, this is reversed (I'm oversimplifying a bit). "I shall die", says the accident victim. "I will die", says the would-be suicide. But what of the pair of them? Shall they die, or will they die? Consider a murder-suicide situation: if *shall* expresses inevitability in the first person and determination in the second and third, and *will* expresses determination in the first and inevitability in the second and third, what will the participants say to one another? "I will die and you will die", cries one. "No, no", says another. "You shall die and I shall die." Actually, he shall die and she will die, or vice versa, depending on who has the gun.

Another reason for the disappearance of the distinction is the use of contractions, and the contraction of *will* and *shall* to *'ll* is one of the most seductive available. Who would fret about whether to write "she shall" or "she will" when she could simply write "she'll" and be unassailable (save by those purists who insist abbreviations have no place in written English)?

This is one I don't get all choked up about, probably because it has been generally ignored on this side of the Atlantic for longer than I can remember, although it has always fallen pleasantly on my ear or eye when reading or listening to people from England, where, I assume, it was taught more enthusiastically than it ever has been here. It is quite refreshing to hear someone say "shall" and to realize that the speaker is making a useful distinction that is seldom respected here.

For my first three years of writing about English usage for *Books in Canada* I cunningly managed to avoid dealing with the subjunctive, and I think I will try to do much the same here. However, this

chapter is about lost causes, and the subjunctive is one of those, so I
can't ignore it entirely. I was drawn into the subject the first time by
a letter from a reader who complained about the increasing use of
would have instead of *had* after the conjunction *if*. I kept shuffling
that letter to the bottom of the pile for months, and still wish I'd
burned it. I have actually read obscure articles, by people who are
supposed to know about such things, claiming that the subjunctive
simply does not exist in English. Had I read these at the right time, I
might have chosen to believe them and saved myself a lot of
trouble.

Fowler makes these points about the subjunctive mood: (1) it is
moribund; (2) it probably never would have been possible to draw
up a satisfactory table of its uses; (3) it's no longer worth trying to
do that; and (4) the only people who use it any more are trying to be
either poetic or pretentious. He's simply telling us to forget it, but
he then goes on for some six columns of type, evidently unable to
follow his own advice.

Quirk *et al.* devote but one of their thousand-odd pages to the
subjunctive, beginning with the statement that "The subjunctive is
not an important category in contemporary English". Their work,
A Grammar of Contemporary English, may be definitive, but it
doesn't fall into the "ready-reference" category. If you nose around
in it, you'll find much more about the subjunctive than there is in
the main article. But I don't suggest you do that unless you have
much more patience than I.

Theodore Bernstein says that most authorities agree that the
subjunctive as a form evidenced by an identifiable verb change is
vanishing in modern English. *He* then goes on for two and a half
pages.

If the subjunctive be dead, it refuses to lie down. I think the
truth is that it is neither dead nor dying; it's just that these authorities wish it were. (You see, now, how both *wish* and *if* simply cry out
for it?) The authorities are being lazy or defeatist in this matter.

They are frightened by the prospect of being asked to be definitive about it but cannot resist picking and poking at it.

I am fond of it. If it come(s) unbidden to my pen or tongue, I do not turn it away. If it seem(s) pretentious, as it does to me in these examples, it will not come unbidden. What I am advising is that you play it by ear, since there are not adequate rules to follow. Even Quirk admits that it is not quite right to say "as it was" when you mean "so to speak", and Bernstein notes, despite the authorities he cites, that anyone who says "if I was you" is going to be classed as illiterate. And Fowler allows that "there are no uses of the subjunctive to which poets, and poetic writers, may not resort if it suits [sic] them". Fowler here eschews the subjunctive and, although no ordinary writer himself, cautions us that "it is no defence for the ordinary writer who uses an antiquated subjunctive to plead that he can parallel it in a good poet".

After pausing to admire the manner in which the writer was sticking to his principles, I gave myself some time to thumb through the book, hoping my eye would fall on some unnecessary or even grandiloquent use of the mood, but what I found instead was this tiny entry under *were*: "For the subjunctive uses in the singular,...some of which are more inconsistent than others with the writing of natural English, see SUBJUNCTIVES." Well, *he* is consistent. But, should it be your choice to go along with him, don't let me catch you saying "be it said" or "if need be" or "far be it from me".

A couple of years ago, I would have been reluctant to call the *lay/lie* distinction a lost cause. I was still accustomed to hearing some Americans and a lot of Canadians saying something like this: "Did I say 'lay'? I think I meant 'lie'. Which is it? Jeez, I can never keep that one straight." As long as people were worrying about it, there was hope. I don't think anyone worries about it any more. It now appears to be entirely acceptable in speech and informal writing (the rest will follow) for "educated" Americans to say "I was laying awake last night, worrying about the decline in literacy". Canadians, as usual, are being quick to follow suit. The progress of this decay has been discernible in the past decade or so to anyone with a sensitive ear or eye.

Lay is almost always a transitive verb. It requires an object. You might lay your cards on the table. If you are a hen, you can lay an egg. If you are a stern parent, you might lay down the law. If you are a lounge lizard, you might lay a broad. There is nothing wrong with beginning a prayer with "Now I lay me down to sleep", since *me* is the object, but you do not lay down to sleep. You *lie* down to sleep. Last night I lay down to sleep, but tonight I shall lie down to sleep.

The catch, of course, is in the other forms of the two verbs. You might say correctly that last night you laid down the law to your children and then lay down for a sleepless night of worrying whether you had been too harsh. Or you could say you laid a memo on my desk two weeks ago and it has lain there, unread, ever since.

The distinction is a bit complicated, but not terribly difficult to learn. The problem is that it is not being taught and not being observed by the speakers and writers who influence us all.

There was a line of dialogue spoken by an attorney in *Love and Hate*, the CBC's drama about the Colin Thatcher murder case: "You were laying in bed at the time you were aroused..." I have no objection to the writer's having put those words into the mouth of a character, and it may have been taken directly from the transcript. That is pretty much the way lawyers talk nowadays. But given the modern sexual connotations of *laying* and *aroused,* I thought the choice of words a trifle distracting in the context.

One of the worst shocks of all my years came on the evening of February 6, 1992, the occasion of the fortieth anniversary of the accession to the Throne of Queen Elizabeth II. I was watching a TV documentary on the daily life of Her Majesty when by ear was jolted by her voice saying "We try and encourage" something or other.

Gawd! The bottom just dropped out of everything. It's *HER LANGUAGE*. She is the Queen. It is called the Queen's English. If *she* can't get it right, what hope is there?

Try and is a vulgar idiom that has been with us for more than a century (Thackeray and Matthew Arnold used it). If I say that I will try *to* improve my syntax, I am promising to make an effort to do so, not promising to succeed in doing so. If I say I will try *and* improve my syntax, I am saying not only that I will make the effort, but that I will succeed. If I am promising to succeed, there is no need to talk of trying. Perhaps *try and* could be useful as a quick way of saying "I will do it, but it will take much effort", but it is not usually used with that intention. It is usually used wrongly in place of the formal *try to,* which is correct and makes sense. It requires less physical effort to say "I'll try 'n' do it" than "I'll try to do it", but that is not a good reason for writing the former. In fact, there is no good reason at all.

Everybody says "I am trying *to* do something". I have never heard anyone say, for example, "I am trying *and* bake a cake". So why should anyone say "I will try and bake a cake"?

This is a distinction that matters. If the finance minister tells us he's going to try to hold the line on taxes, he is expressing good intentions, but it doesn't mean he won't hit us with an increase. If he says he will try *and* hold the line, he's damn' well promised to do it. If more opposition politicians understood the distinction, they'd have a lot of ammunition in debate.

The most compelling reason for my loathing for the term is that it doesn't make any sense. There are many things in English that don't make sense, but, in a sense, there are many that do, and *try to* is one of them. I have to confess to being stopped cold once in a discussion of this with the writer and editor Doug Marshall. I told him that I could die happy — or even happily — if I could convince the English-speaking peoples to stick with *try to*, and never, under any circumstances, say *try and*. Said Doug, who can be merciless: "You'll try and fail."

A similar annoyance is *different than*, which doesn't make any more sense than *try and*, but which has been widely used for about three centuries. It is a true lost cause. It bothers me, but I don't expect much sympathy. One reason for its wide acceptance is that in many constructions it takes fewer words than does the "correct" *different from*. I might say "My assessment of the importance of this distinction is different from yours" without being tempted to use *than*, but I admit it's easier to say "I followed a different method than the cookbook recommended" than "I followed a different method from the one the cookbook recommended". When I see *than*, I simply can't keep from looking for a comparative adjective or adverb, and *different(ly)* doesn't qualify.

Other than that, I have nothing to say. I won't even mention the British *different to*, except to note that Fowler says it's okay (well, okay, *he* wouldn't say "okay") to use it, and that its prohibition is another "superstition". That's okay with me, although I don't know why anyone would want to say that, but anyone who repeatedly says *different than* is not welcome in my bar, and that includes all the heads, past and present, of this and other states who do it all the time. I don't give a hoot for all the exalted precedents quoted in the *OED*; *different than* is illogical, even though it is sometimes difficult to work around. It is never a waste of time to apply the test of logic to language problems.

Possibly there is no point in continuing to fight the treatment of *media* as though it were singular. I have never heard a valid argument for treating it that way, but the misuse is supported by many writers who should know better.

Medium has many meanings. In this context, it is a noun identifying a means or instrument of communication, and the preferred plural is *media*. Newspapers and magazines used to be our main sources of news. They were the news media. When radio and television gained strength in this area, they, too, became news media, so newspapers and magazines became the print media. Then everything got lumped together as the mass media. Eventually, all these things were becoming, simply, the media, and that's when the trouble started. Nurtured by egocentric and sloppy journalists, *the media* took on a life of its own as a way of identifying the news media, and no attention was paid to the fact that there are many other media. Television and radio are mass media, but they are not themselves part of *the media*; only their news divisions qualify for that.

It was inevitable, then, that *the media* would come to be regarded as identifying a single entity, and that *media* would be treated as a singular noun. It was only a short step to the appearance of *medias*.

Not long ago, I read, in a news item about preparations for an international conference, "There will be more than 350 media there". I was pleased that *media*, not *medias*, was used, but it wouldn't have mattered. I still don't know if the reporter meant 350 representatives of various media or the representatives of 350 news media organizations or 350 dishes of agar, which, as every schoolboy knows, is a cultural medium.

Ilk is a Scottish word that does not mean kind or set or family. It means same. *Of that ilk* identifies people from a property of the same name. There is a city in England named Blackburn, and I suppose there are Blackburns of that ilk, but I am not one of them. *Ilk* is of so little use in English that there probably is no serious harm in its widespread misuse, but there is no reason to misuse it. You could live a pretty full life without ever finding a reason to use it properly. Most misuses stem from the notion that *ilk* is a cute variation of *like*: "pedants and others of that ilk" or "bigots and their ilk". To use it in such ways is to flaunt ignorance.

I think people who say "if I would have" done this or that (or, worse, "if I would *of*") have misunderstood speakers who said "if I were to have done...". At any rate, they're wrong. A simple "if I had" or even "had I" would suffice.

There are some causes that I believe to be lost to which I say good riddance. One is the cause of those who would forbid us to start a sentence with a conjunction. I don't know if this is still being taught, but I have several friends who had it drummed into them so effectively in school that they are absolutely bloody-minded about it. They will condemn a writer out of hand simply on the basis of spotting a conjunction that begins with a capital letter. This is just foolish. A conjunction is one of a set of words used to connect clauses *or sentences.* You can go back to the *OED* or to any respectable newer dictionary for confirmation of that. I have no idea who dreamed up the nonsensical idea that it is improper to use a conjunction to conjoin sentences (obviously it was not someone who had ever even glanced at the glorious collection of writings known as the King James Bible), but I would like to see it laid to rest.

CHAPTER 7

Dots and Dashes & Other Small Pests

You might ask, reasonably, how I can rant on about adherence to rules and guidelines while I am patently playing fast and loose with all the cherished laws of punctuation. Obviously, some of the punctuation used in this book will strike some as being a bit on the oddball side. This is particularly apparent in the matter of, to put it simply, whether the period comes before or after the closing quotation mark. I have spent many years doing battle, from time to time, with many editors, over this issue. I always lose, not because I am wrong, but because they have the last say and because they cherish their traditions. They think nothing of shifting a correctly placed period from the outside to the inside because "that's the style". It's the style for no reason other than the conceit that it looks better. Perhaps it does look better. What's more, especially to the North American eye, it looks *right*, simply because it has become the conventional style. That's a mean, if not downright vicious, circle.

Fowler, who, in the manner of his countrymen, prefers to call quotation marks inverted commas, has this to say:

There are two schools of thought, which might be called the

conventional and the logical. The conventional prefers to put stops within the inverted commas, if it can be done without ambiguity, on the ground that this has a more pleasing appearance. The logical punctuates according to sense, and puts them outside except when they actually form part of the quotation.

Fowler of course favours the logical, as we all should. He allows that in some constructions (for instance, where logic would require a period on each side of a quotation mark) "logic must respect appearances". But he says in conclusion: "The conventional system flouts common sense, and it is not easy for the plain man to see what merit it has to outweigh that defect; even the more pleasing appearance claimed for it is not likely to go unquestioned."

The heart of the problem is to be found in that phrase "if it can be done without ambiguity". (Note that Fowler is merely describing the convention, not condoning it.)

There are many editors who will exercise that sort of discretion. There are many more, though, who will not; who will blindly follow the convention no matter what damage it wreaks on the sense of the text. To license the conditional flouting of rules is to invite trouble, but the majority of publishers do it. They are like the benighted teachers who tell their pupils that spelling and grammar don't matter as long as they can get their ideas across, thereby infesting the world with a generation of people who follow every statement with "You know what I mean?". Usually the appropriate reply is no.

Cosmetic (my own term for what Fowler calls conventional) punctuation bothers me chiefly because it is illogical, but I use it in most of my writing, knowing that logical punctuation is certain to be changed before publication, possibly in a way that will pervert my meaning. If it must be wrong, I prefer to make it wrong in my own way. There's little satisfaction in having someone else commit your sins for you.

A simple bit of advice for anyone foolhardy enough to try to use quotation marks rationally: assuming that you know the rules for placing stops within or outside parentheses, apply them to quotation marks.

To some extent, I regret my decision to try to follow the logical system in these pages. It's made for a lot of extra work, and I'm sure I've nodded here and there and lapsed into the typing habits I developed in school and in my early newspaper days. I've made many efforts over the years to sneak what I consider correct punctuation past editorial eyes and into print, and sometimes been successful, but the opportunity to practise what I have preached in a book of my own had to be grasped.

Another deviation I have indulged myself in is non-standard use of italics. Most publishers in Canada use quotation marks to indicate that a word is being used out of context. In a book of this sort, these marks would cause a serious amount of eyestrain. I have adapted (but not fully adopted) some of the practices used by Fowler in *A Dictionary of Modern English Usage* in an effort to mitigate that problem. Perhaps I have been a bit inconsistent here and there — there are borderline cases in which I have made arbitrary decisions.

There are, I think, too few such devices as italics. In my early newspaper days, the rank-and-file were denied the use of italics, although the device was available to the editorial-page writers in the ivory tower. All that was available to the lower echelons was boldface type, and that was used indiscriminately for cosmetic purposes by the news editors — every third paragraph or so would be set bold, just to break up the greyness of the standard typeface. Subheads were used in the same way, and were placed at fairly regular intervals, whether the context called for one or not. Usually they

were meaningless. Much of this sort of thing still goes on. Boldface
could be used for emphasis, but its cosmetic use interfered with the
effectiveness. Italics are much more readily available now, but other
devices, such as SMALL CAPITALS, still are hard to come by. Regular capitals can be used for screaming, but are intrusive and tend to
be confused with acronyms. For what little remains of the lifespan
of the printed word, some new typographical conventions should
be established to enable us to go out in style.

Poets and writers of fiction are artists. They are entitled to be creative in their use of punctuation marks. They may be condemned
for doing it badly, of course. It's pretty easy to tell whether the
unorthodox punctuation in creative work is the result of crafts-
manship or ignorance. Some years ago when I first sampled the
wares of the Irish novelist J.P. Donleavy, I was quite taken by his
writing, and quite prepared to tolerate his relentless practice of
writing in half-sentences. But, after a couple of books, it began to
grate on my nerves, and finally I abandoned him for that reason
only. The creative punctuator must take that risk.
    I assume that most people who can read at all have some knowl-
edge of what the various punctuation marks are for, or that they at
least will respond to them with some fairly predictable subcon-
scious reactions, and I use the marks accordingly. I don't think this
makes me a punctuation anarchist. I respect the rules, but bend
them to suit my purposes.
    I like the *RH-II*'s simple definition of *punctuate*: "To mark or
divide (something written) with punctuation marks in order to
make the meaning clear." (Mind you, I wouldn't object to a comma
at the obvious place in that sentence, but the meaning was clear.) It
becomes a bit more complicated when it comes to *punctuation,*
which is defined: "The practice or system of using certain conventional marks or characters in writing or printing in order to

separate elements and make the meaning clear, as in ending a sentence or separating clauses."

One needs to know a little more than that, but it's good to keep in mind. The marks (and the purposes they serve) are a matter of convention, and the aim is clarity. That leaves a lot of leeway, but I would not encourage any beginning writer to take advantage of it. There are simple and succinct guides to the elements of punctuation, and they should be studied and reviewed. One of the best to keep around is *Strunk & White*. Don't mess with the rules until you know them.

The apostrophe serves two important functions, neither of which is to make a noun plural. One is to indicate a contraction, the other is to form a possessive.

It is not necessary to memorize a lot of rules to know that it is not usual to form the plural of pronouns by adding S, so an apostrophe is not necessary to indicate the possessive. The plural of *it* is not *its*; it's *them*, and so on. It doesn't hurt to bear in mind that the smallness of apostrophes does *not* justify squandering them. They should not be used, either, to form plurals, save to avoid confusion. This decade, for example, is the 1990s, not the 1990's.

There is an interesting problem in the world of computers, wherein we find the very common term *DOS*. *DOS*, pronounced "doss", is an acronym for disk operating system. The plural is *DOSs*, but since many computer programs in some circumstances change everything to upper case, no matter what you type, and would change *DOSs* to *DOSS*, those who use the beasts often write *DOSES* as the plural, despite the unsavoury connotation. Since *doss* is a word (albeit not one that is on everyone's lips nowadays), it would be inappropriate to use *DOSS* for the plural of *DOS*. In this case, *DOS'S* might be permissible. But what happens if you are comparing several such systems? Should you refer to some of these

DOS'S'S advantages over other DOS'S? I think not; rather you should thank God for *of.*

If you are a signpainter, you should heed Fowler's admonition: "To insert an apostrophe in the plural of an ordinary noun is a fatuous vulgarism." You should, however, dot your *i's* and cross your *t's* and mind your *p's* and *q's.*

I once wrote a piece, for a general-interest magazine, that brought me a letter from some pedant who informed me that contractions have no place in written English. This led me to wonder why God gave us the apostrophe. Perhaps it was His intention that we use it only to denote the genitive case, but since possession is almost a dirty word in many religions, I wondered why he would provide us with a tool to serve no other purpose than to indicate possession. The use of this tiny scratch to indicate a contraction must have some justification, and, since it is a written symbol, where in hell else would you use it save in written English?

Perhaps contractions do not belong in formal English, but they're indispensable to a writer who's trying to communicate with a large body of readers through the popular press by adopting a conversational tone — something I often try to do. It shows up, for example, when I write *damn'* instead of *damned.* I suppose it's a damn' bad habit, but I'm damned if I can break it.

I wonder if it is fear of pedants that drives so many writers and editors to use apostrophes where they do not belong. There is a superabundance of apostrophes, and if they cannot — sorry, if they can not — be used to indicate contractions, and if possession is a sin, what is to be done with them? Many editors feel they should be used before an S to indicate a plural, as in 1980's, or Emmy's or the Jones's. They are wrong. Many other stray apostrophes end up being used to create such abominations as "their's", "her's", "our's", and the ubiquitous "it's". (*Its,* of course, is the correct spelling of the possessive; *it's* is the correct way to write the contraction of *it is*. But I have forgotten — we must not write contractions.)

At any rate, the apostrophe probably is the most widely and frequently misused of all the marks. I have seen conscientious newspaper editors become quite demented by the frustration of being unable to train their writers to remember that *it's* is a contraction of *it is* and *its* is the possessive of *it*. This is surely the simplest of distinctions, yet the pages of our daily newspapers are riddled with examples of this error. It is not by accident that I've mentioned it more than once in these pages. It's a worthy cause. Were the dream of some bureaucrats to be realized we would have another CBC. Then there would be two CBCs, not two CBC's.

Finally, if you are an etymological purist, you will pronounce *apostrophe* (when referring to the punctuation mark, not to the figure of speech) with only three syllables, but you will feel very lonely.

I have always had a hellish time with commas, and things have gotten worse over the years. Not only do different editors have different ideas, but styles change. There are fewer commas around today than when I was a lad. The "tough" writers of the 1920s and 1930s had a lot to do with this. There seemed to be a dictum: real men don't use commas. Perhaps the comma should be placed on the endangered species list. There may be a movement to do away with it entirely. It is true that if you follow the old rules you sometimes end up with more commas than are absolutely necessary for clarity, but newspaper editors have gone too far in cutting out the ones they deem to be superfluous. The result has been a sort of syntactic anarchy, and the ensuing chaos is not mitigated by any simpleminded instruction to "punctuate for sense". That is certainly not a good thing to say to anyone who has not yet caught the sense of the rudiments of punctuation.

The writer who punctuates by the rules does both himself and his reader a service. If he knows the rules he can do it automatically, and is less likely to be misunderstood. If he "punctuates for sense", he has to keep stopping to think about it, and even then is likely to blow it, and the reader may not have discerned what he is up to. On the other hand, I am convinced that it is necessary for today's writer sometimes to eschew slavish devotion to the long-established rules to communicate effectively. "Punctuate *with* sense" might be a better directive.

I found an example of one of the pitfalls of messing with the rules when I was stopped dead by a passage in Richard Gwyn's *The Northern Magus*: "Later, Trudeau's ideas would change. But for about four years, he preached and practised the doctrine of national self-interest." I read *but for* in the sense of with the exception of, and took the opposite meaning from the one Gwyn intended. The hell of all this is that *Strunk & White* has a general rule that would condone Gwyn's omission of a comma after *but,* but, in this case, the omission led to confusion. The omission of commas is supposed, by the omitters, to remove unnecessary impediments to the flow of their words; too often it has the opposite effect. A smooth flow is of no value if it leads the reader away from the writer's stream of thought and forces him to go back and reread.

I admit to a cavalier attitude toward the comma: I have paid my dues and studied the rules, and I'll put commas where I damn' well want them. For example, as you may have noticed, I don't see any need to insert a comma before all quotations in the conventional way. Some editor might say, "You must do it this way," and I say "I'm damned if I will". Most such commas are superfluous, and no harm is done by omitting them judiciously.

One trap that the enthusiastic omitter of commas falls into is the failure to recognize situations in which they must come in pairs. That might seem obvious, but the more comma-free the prose, the more common the flaws. It is necessary to recognize situations in which you have a choice of whether to put one *here* and to know that, if you do, you must also put one *there*. A good example of the importance of this is involved in the proper observation of the *that/which* distinction, which is discussed in Chapter 12. Unfortunately, it is a distinction that most people, maybe even most writers, don't understand. But to observe it, you must not only know when to use *that* and when to use *which*, but also recognize that which requires commas (or that *which* requires commas).

I recall an absolutely ridiculous exchange of letters with a would-be writer who had been taking a zany assortment of writing courses for years. Her current teacher was death on commas, and I tried to explain that they could often be left out if the omissions were done judiciously. I suggested that the correct insertion of commas was a matter of craft, but their omission is an art. That fell on deaf ears (or, I suppose, on blind eyes, if you want to be finicky about it). She later reported (*crowed* would be more accurate) that she had tried to follow my suggestions in a piece she had submitted to some sort of trade publication and said the editor had told her she was using too many commas. I had seen the publication in question, and noted that nothing in it showed any signs of having been edited at all. I asked to see what she had written, and, as I had suspected, the problem was not simply the large number of commas but the fact that they seemed to have been sprinkled on with a pepper grinder rather than placed.

There is always a lot of argument about serial commas: when you want to say "My favourite foods are raw carrots, fried rice, tofu, and foie gras", do you need that comma after *tofu*? My answer is that you certainly do, and I'll cite *Strunk & White* as my authority. Others disagree, but the convention of the comma before *and* is useful in avoiding possible confusion, and the cost is negligible.

Someone once wrote me to propound a theory that the main trouble with commas is that they curve the wrong way, cupping, as it were, the reader's eye, and thus impeding the flow. Printing them backward, he suggested, would make them less disruptive but still able to serve their purpose.

That might be a good idea, but it does not seem likely to be accepted overnight. Meanwhile, why not give some thought to the lowly dash? Its use is decried by some purists, but it is a valuable tool. Although it is defined as a stronger stop than the comma, the eye slides easily along it, and it is certainly less disruptive than the round bracket when used to enclose parenthetical material. In a sentence full of commas performing other functions, it is some-times unfair to make them serve also as symbols of parenthesis, and — presuming you do not wish to use as arresting a sign as the round bracket — the dash serves admirably (save in some cases in which a further stop is required immediately after you close your parentheses).

One problem with using dashes in writing for publication is that some typesetters seem unable to understand that there is a dif-ference between a dash and a hyphen.

Shorten the dash by half and you have one of the language's greatest trouble-makers — the hyphen. A dissertation on its use and misuse could go on too long. The most concise advice is to avoid it when-ever possible. Sir Winston Churchill, who did not care for the hyphen, suggested that "you may run [words] together or leave them apart, except when nature revolts". The fact is that nature revolts quite often. For one thing, a nine-year-old boy is not nine-years-old, he is nine years old. If that seems obvious to you, it nevertheless is obviously not obvious to a great many newspaper writers and editors.

Hyphens, like commas, are the subject of many rules that need not be slavishly adhered to but should be understood and consid-ered. One situation in which hyphens are particularly desirable is the formation of a compound adjective used before the noun it is modifying. The anti-hyphen activists would say that you don't have to follow this rule, but I can't buy that. For example, a first-class lesson is not the same thing as a first class lesson. A silent movie fan is not the same as a silent-movie fan.

I have a lot of trouble with the semicolon, but take comfort in the knowledge that I am not alone. The main rule is that if you have two clauses that could stand alone as sentences, they should be separated by a semicolon. You see it used so seldom in non-professional writing that I suspect a great many readers do not know what it's for and may even be confused by it. It makes sense that it is a bit more of an eye-stopper than is the comma, since that's its function. It's a useful stop, and it's a pity that about all it's used for now is to separate items in a list when some of the items already contain commas.

Since the colon has fallen into disuse as a stop, it has acquired, as Fowler puts it, "a special function: that of delivering the goods that have been invoiced in the preceding words". Unfortunately, that new function effectively buries the old one, because the modern reader will, on seeing a colon, expect what follows to be a fulfillment of the promise that preceded it. Its old function as a stop is often served well by the multi-purpose dash or a full stop, but it is still pleasant to see it used occasionally in the way God intended.

Since punctuation is not intrusively apparent to the consumer of broadcast information, people know less and less about it. Paragraphing is perhaps the lostest of the lost arts of punctuation.

I have a mental quirk that I was not aware of until recently: when I am listening critically, I have a tendency to mentally type the prose I am hearing, inserting punctuation marks as I go along. I can see the output on a mental screen or sheet of paper. When I became aware of it, I assumed it was the result of writing habits developed during years of writing columns and features (as opposed to news stories). It was my wont (often to the annoyance of my fellow slaves) to pace about the office, cracking my knuckles, while mentally composing my next sentence, on the completion of which I would rush back to my typewriter, bumping into chairs and wastebaskets to rattle it off before it faded away. Another possible factor is that during the early days I was much in demand to take dictation over the phone, being a reasonably spry typist and good speller. This may be a chicken-or-egg matter. Whatever, I find it an interesting phenomenon. I am glad I can switch it on and off — particularly off.

When it is on, it can handle all the punctuation marks, but it's weak on paragraphing, and so am I. The only instruction about paragraphing that a young reporter is likely to get is "Keep 'em short". I have no quarrel with that. Most readers, including me, tend to shy away from paragraphs that look formidably bulky and dense, and I don't see much wrong in breaking them up for cosmetic reasons. Anyway, I learned that simple lesson, and that's about all I ever did learn about paragraphing. I know that the main rule is that a paragraph break should indicate a greater change of subject than does a sentence break, but I don't think it's anything to get worked up about.

Moulding paragraphs is not great fun, but sentences are another matter. I am one of many people who occasionally take delight in writing sentences of several hundred words, and I have been able to sneak a number of them into print, which is no small trick on a major daily newspaper. There's no joy in long paragraphs.

CHAPTER 8

Caught Between Cultures

I have no wish to make a big deal about this book being Canadian. It was written and published in Canada by a Canadian writer and a Canadian publisher, and that's enough. A lot of people, particularly in television and movies, try to make their work "distinctively Canadian" out of some misguided attempt to be patriotic or get government grants. A lot of other Canadians, particularly in television and movies, try to make their work distinctively American — or at least attempt to disguise the fact that it's Canadian — out of an understandable desire to make a decent buck. Neither of these approaches works very well very often.

There are some unique aspects to writing — and reading — in Canada. We have been caught between two cultures. The English speak *the Queen's English* (which was *the King's English* when I was learning it) and the Americans speak *the American Language,* which existed long before H.L. Mencken identified it. I don't think there is any such thing as Canadian English or "the Canadian Language" (or even "the Prime Minister's English", thank God). There are merely some characteristics that make both the British and the Americans think that we "talk funny".

I consider it my good fortune that much, perhaps most, of my pre-teen reading, largely guided by my WASP mother, came from England: boys' magazines such as *Champion* and *Triumph* and *Boys' Own Magazine* and the annuals they all published, and even comic books, such as *Crackers*. I still remember the adventures of the likes of the detective Colwyn Dane and every schoolboy's dream of the ideal schoolmaster, Fireworks Flynn. And there was Rockfist Rogan, the pugilist and RAF fighter pilot, who, in 1939, performed the greatest of his many superhuman feats by moving from World War I to World War II without aging a day. There were the Henty books, and *Tom Brown's Schooldays*, then Edgar Wallace and *Sherlock Holmes* and much more. I had a lot of this under my belt before I discovered Mark Twain and the American comic books and pulp magazines, and that foundation was enough to keep me reading British as well as American works and to welcome Dickens and Shakespeare in high school. I suppose I missed a lot of what my American cousins (that's not a figure of speech: I had ten first cousins growing up in Boston) were reading. I don't recall being exposed to Zane Grey, but then I'll bet they didn't read the Biggles books.

At any rate, looking back now, I know I was exposed to a great deal of both American and British literature, and that both influences are evident, at least to me, in my speech and writing. It bothers me that I tend to accept this as what it is to be a Canadian (of my generation, at least), because I'm damned if I can remember reading any Canadian books as a kid, either at home or at school, and I was well along in my teens before I had any real awareness that there *were* such things — and quite a few of them at that. Their authors, I assume, were subject to the same effect of being caught between two "foreign" cultures, yet were writing as Canadians, and I wish I had been exposed to them earlier. I have never come close to catching up.

(In passing: There is a fine book, *Wordstruck*, by the eminent journalist Robert MacNeil, in which he reminisces about growing up literate in Canada. I recommend it.)

So I was taught at home and at school to honour traditional British spellings. When I went into newspaper work, I had to learn to honor Canadian newspaper style, which, for the most part, simply meant U.S. style. At *The Ottawa Journal*, every *-our* ending became *-or*, save in the case of *Saviour*, and only the one with the capital S; *savior* was okay. So much of the content of the newspapers came from U.S. wire services and syndicates that it was simpler (meaning cheaper) to follow certain of their conventions than the ones we had grown up with.

Canadian writers and editors must cope every day with assorted problems related to their situation in a major market for the outpourings of the U.S. media.

I know at least one editor who froths at the mouth at the sight or sound of *loan* used as a verb, arguing that *loan* is the noun, *lend* is the verb, and that asking someone to loan you his lawn mower is a vulgar Americanism.

The fact is that *loan* was current in England as a verb for centuries. It was eventually replaced by *lend*, but, before that happened, *loan* had been carried by English settlers to the United States and had taken root there. Its use in that country is unexceptionable, and, given the degree to which Canadian writers have embraced U.S. idiom, we cannot say flatly that it is wrong.

It is, however, wholly unnecessary in any country. It has crept back into England, where Fowler's successors still term it a "needless variation", and it doubtless will outlive us all. I find it has a disagreeable ring. It is widely used on television talk shows by people who give the impression that they believe it lends an air of elegance to their speech. You may, if you wish, deride their pretentiousness, but they are within their rights.

It would be good if all Canadian editors shared my friend's ambition to stamp out the verb *loan,* but such action can be justified on grounds of taste only, not propriety. And, considering the real errors that riddle our speech and writing, such a crusade should not be given the highest priority. I'd prefer, for example, to see a slaughter of sportscasters who say things like "He's hurtin' real good".

One more item on *loan*: *The Toronto Sun* evidently has decided not only that *loan* is a verb, but also that it means borrow. That may seem incredible, but I have the clipping from an article on household security precautions: "Loan an engraver from your local police station", it advises. And after you've done that, you'd better loan a dictionary from your local borrowing library.

I have known more than one newspaper editor who, whenever he saw a reporter consulting the big newsroom dictionary, would holler "If you don't know what it means, don't use it".

If we accept the view entertained by some newspaper publishers that most of their readers are semiliterate, we must regard that as sound advice. However, it has unfortunate side-effects. When I see an error committed by a writer (other than a news writer under deadline pressure), I assume that he or she was either too lazy to consult a reference or too ignorant to recognize the possibility of error. Perhaps I should add a third possibility: fear of being seen looking something up.

Such reflections tempered my initial enthusiasm over the publication in 1985, by Dundurn Press, of *The Canadian Style,* a stylebook prepared by the Department of the Secretary of State as a guide to writing and editing. It is primarily for civil servants, but is on public sale.

I suppose my knee-jerk response on hearing of this was

commonplace: surely any such work, prepared by and for government employees, would be an endorsement of bureaucratese, written in gobbledygook. Anyone accustomed to government documents could be excused for having such prejudice. In fact, though,
it is an excellent 250-page compendium of sound advice that, if followed by all, would enable us to understand each other. That would
be a nice change.

However, having a good stylebook available and making use of
it are different things. Most offices in which writing is done have
dictionaries available, but spelling errors persist. What reason have
we to believe that a writer who is too stupid or lazy to look up a
word in a dictionary is likely to undertake the rather more complex
task of consulting a stylebook or a usage guide?

Big newspapers have their own stylebooks, and most of the ones
I've worked for always had a gnome locked somewhere in a dusty
closet writing a new one. One of the most respected stylebooks
through the years has been that of the Canadian Press. As I said earlier, that news agency gave birth to Broadcast News (it is now Standard Broadcast News, but nothing seems to have changed), whose
output has been read aloud hourly on countless radio stations for
decades and scrolls endlessly up the TV screens of cable subscribers
across the country. I have sometimes held up the BN service as one
of the most visible examples of atrocious writing. (It also has certain other weaknesses as a news medium. One Christmas time, one
of its top news headlines of one day was POPE WANTS CHRISTIANS
TO LEAD GODLY LIVES. What a scoop that was!) The BN writers
certainly had access to the CP stylebook, but there is little evidence
that any of them actually used it.

There are, however, reasons to feel encouraged by the publication of *The Canadian Style*. I find it gratifying (and not a little
astonishing) to discover that there are people with some power in
the civil service who are not only concerned about the calibre of

English used by their employees but also capable of producing a guide of this quality. Having done so, their next responsibility should be to enforce observance of the standards they have set.

Doubtless some worriers will regard the distribution of this book outside the government service as evidence of creeping linguistic big-brotherism, but it seems unlikely to me, even in the post-1984 era, that there is anything sinister in this. I am simply grateful for the book, and would like to see one in every home, not just in every office. It does not, after all, have the power of law.

But within the civil service, the same people who ordered the production of the guide surely have the authority to insist that it be followed by public servants who are paid to write.

I once had some dealings with an editor transplanted here from the U.S. He didn't exactly endear himself to everyone by constantly muttering that Canadians can't spell. That may be true in a sense — one could claim with equal justification that Americans can't spell, either. What he meant, though, was simply that he couldn't adjust to the differences in spelling between the two countries, and my answer to him was that if Canadians can't spell, then Americans can't count.

At the end of 1983, the newspapers and newscasts gave wide circulation to the story of an American bon vivant who had just made a hotel reservation for the December 31, 1999, New Year's Eve celebration, because he wanted to make sure he would be able to greet the twenty-first century in proper style.

Not one of the stories I saw or heard mentioned the fact that the man was a year off in his timing, probably because maybe about 99.9 percent of the population would think he was right.

This amazes me, because anyone who thinks about it must recognize that the twenty-first century will begin on January 1,

2001, *not* 2000. That is plain *fact*, and anyone who disputes it is
being illogical.

In our calendar, there is no year zero. The first century of the
Christian era began on January 1 of the year 1 A.D. This century
began on January 1, 1901. The next century will begin on January 1,
2001. It's that simple.

The prevalence of this misconception drove me to distraction in
1949 and 1950, when there was a tremendous foofaraw about our
entering the second half of this century in 1950, when in fact we
remained in the first half throughout that year. And all that hulla-
baloo surely will be as nothing compared with what's going to start
happening in 1999, provided the world survives that long. I don't
expect to be here for it, and that's just as well, because I think the
frustration of trying to make my point would kill me anyway.

So I'm bringing it up now, in the hope that a few of you will put
it in the backs of your minds and carry on the fight when the time
comes.

Should any of you think that this subject is a little off-topic here,
I disagree. Numbers are part of our language. And this misuse of
them is identical to the misuse of words — it stems from wrong
thinking and the failure of the mass media to impose discipline on
the so-called communicators upon whom we rely so heavily.

Probably this particular misconception is so generally accepted
because of our common way of labelling our decades as *the Twenties* or *the 1930s* or *the '40s*, and so on. This is colloquial and convenient, and I have no quarrel with it on those grounds, although it is
misleading. It would be pointless to say that 1980 was not the first
year of *the '80s*, but the fact remains that it was the last year of the
seventh decade of this century, not the first of the eighth. Anyone
who thinks of decades in the colloquial terminology could be pardoned for having to stop and think before realizing that the last
year of the 1990s is *not* the last year of the twentieth century, but

should not be pardoned for failing to stop and think before publishing the misinformation.

The problem may also have something to do with North American impatience, which also shows up in the peculiar way in which the logical system of decimal counting in the U.S., and hence in Canada, becomes illogical when it passes from 999,999,999 to 1,000,000,000. The latter number is not one billion, it is one thousand million, as the British well know. One billion is 1,000,000,000,000. This is where impatience and megalomania come in. Everything has to be bigger and faster in the U.S. They can't wait to become billionaires, and they can't wait to enter new eras. If the Olympic Games were controlled by the United States, I have no doubt that the athletes would be contending for platinum medals, not gold.

We read that there are many billionaires (in terms of the Canadian or U.S. dollar) in the world. Actually there isn't one. Properly, a man would have to be worth a million million dollars to be called that, and I can't think offhand of anyone who qualifies. If there were, he would popularly be called a trillionaire, but to merit *that* label he actually would have to be worth $1,000,000,000,000,000,000. And that's a lot of bread.

Such vast numbers have little reality for most of us. But consider that it's exactly the same as if North Americans had decided somewhere along the line that the number after nine would be called one hundred, or that ten times ten would be called one thousand. It is, simply, that illogical.

(Of course, it cuts both ways. I'm sure that there are times the Americans would prefer to think of the potential perils posed by a mere thousand million Chinese rather than a billion of them.)

So, just as we are impatient to turn our millionaires into billionaires, we seem impatient to get from one century to the next; so impatient that we will be agreeable to stupidly believing that we are in the next one a year before the current one has ended.

When all the noisy nonsense is going on in 1999, I hope with all my heart that there will be one among those who read this who will stand up and holler "But the Emperor is bare-ass nekkid, and he ain't no billionaire, neither!". I am assuming, of course, that by then such a sentence will be considered to be good English.

The delightful international English-language quarterly *Verbatim* once ran a piece by Brian Cahill of Ottawa comparing British and Canadian newspaper writing. He quoted the following excerpt from an editorial-page column in *The Globe and Mail*:

> Allan MacEachen, Hecate-like, whispers a beguiling exorcism into the trembling ears of the Liberal Party's platform committee on the weekend, 48 hours before two by-election votes, neither of which the party has a hope of winning. No need to be spooked by Brian Mulroney, the Deputy Prime Minister incants. Right. Not until Birnam wood comes to Dunsinane hill. Besides the Prime Minister's office has moved to a political war-footing.

He then quoted "a similarly-intentioned paragraph" from the London *Sunday Telegraph*:

> Neil Kinnock would seem to be the best choice to lead Labour towards its historic destiny as a minor tourist attraction. He gives the impression that he believes most of the rubbish he talks and it is certainly not his fault that he has the face of an incontinent schoolboy.

As political put-downs go, the winner clearly is the latter excerpt, and I think Cahill was fair enough in his selection of samples (there were several more). His conclusion: "Good English still flourishes in Great Britain and to me this presages the resurrection rather than the death of English in America."

I can only guess why he said America, since he had been talking about Canada, but no matter. It made me start thinking of the persistent delusion that the reason the mother tongue is in decline in English-speaking Canada is our proximity to the United States. The theory is that Canadian English in the twentieth century has been corrupted by the invasion of our culture by the United States media. There may be some truth in this insofar as the infiltration of certain American peculiarities goes, but I have a problem with it. If our linguistic malaise is a result of excessive exposure to American English, why is our writing so often inferior to the United States product?

You may say this is not so, and I am not about to argue. I'm making a subjective judgment, and can't attempt here to support it except by inviting you to make some comparisons on your own between *Time* and *Maclean's*, between *The New Yorker* and *Toronto Life*, between any of the good grey American dailies and *The Globe and Mail*, or between similar U.S. and Canadian specialized magazines in any field. It is my opinion that, in general terms, the writing in Canadian publications and broadcasting services is sloppier than that in their U.S. counterparts, even though the standards of the latter are declining steadily. Believing this, I tend to be leery of claims that the Yanks have been, and are, gravely corrupting our written language. I am talking here about writing for print. I don't think that the English of Canadian broadcasters is any worse than that of their American counterparts.

I am encouraged by what I perceive to be a trend in the way we address certain of our officials. Not so many years ago, it was common to say Mr. Prime Minister, Mr. Minister, Mr. Chief Justice, Mr. Ambassador and so on. Today, judging by the way such people are

addressed on television, the *mister* is going out of use in this context. It was an American aberration. Although it is said that George
Washington craved a majestic honorific, he was overruled, and
everyone became a mister, and it became *de rigueur* to say Mr. President, Mr. Secretary, etc., just as in post-revolutionary France and
Russia it was, respectively, Citizen and Comrade. Here we seem to
have reverted to the British mode, and I consider that a small step in
the right direction. I notice, though, that our MPs still address the
chair as Mr. (or Madam) Speaker (or Monsieur or Madame),
although they can't make up their minds whether the speaker is
l'orateur or *le président.*

For some reason, Americans find our spelling of *cheque* nothing
short of hilarious. That they might find it quaint is understandable,
but it seems to inspire hoots of derision. About forty years ago, the
Newspaper Guild chapter I belonged to in Ottawa sent a contribution to the brothers in New York who were on strike. Our cheque
was acknowledged in a union newsletter with some sort of snide
remark to the effect that it would be accepted despite our ignorance
of spelling. I wanted my share of the donation back.

I once got involved in a ludicrous exchange over the
check/cheque issue. One Eric Elstone wrote me from Acton,
Ontario, that he had achieved a modest triumph in a lengthy battle
between him and the editors of the Canadian edition of *Reader's
Digest.*

The story began in August, 1983. Elstone spotted, in the Canadian edition of *Reader's Digest,* one of those filler items that make
the magazine so popular in places in which people find themselves
forced to sit quietly for brief periods with little external stimulation
for the mind. It reprinted a sentence from Richard Needham's column in *The Globe and Mail*: "If it's a bill, the posties will get it to
you in 24 hours; if it's a check, allow them a couple of weeks."

Elstone thought it unlikely that Needham would spell *cheque* in this way, and wrote the magazine a polite letter urging that it adopt the common Canadian spelling. The senior staff editor Alexander Farrell replied that he could not agree that usage in Canada favoured *cheque* and that *check* was the magazine's entrenched style. He said that *check* was very common in Canada and that there was no clear evidence that *cheque* was the preferred spelling. Elstone challenged this, and Farrell replied in May that Elstone did, after all, appear to be right; that, on further study, it did seem that *cheque* was the preferred spelling. A revision of style was being considered, he said, but he could offer no assurance that the Canadian edition would change its style. Finally, on September 26, Farrell wrote to Elstone saying "You'll be pleased to know that we are adopting the spelling 'cheque' as of our December issue".

That was a happy ending, but it wasn't the whole story. While the correspondence was still flying, I had jumped in with a column in *Books in Canada* in which I wrote: "Surely, you would think, anyone living or working or dealing with Canadians would know, even if he knew nothing else, that, no two ways about it, to a Canadian a cheque is one thing and a check is another." Then I had to go and throw in a wisecrack: "I would, though, like to ask Mr. Elstone what he was doing reading *Reader's Digest* in the first place." I suppose it was a cheap shot, but, what the hell, *everybody* makes jokes about *Reader's Digest*, and people go on buying it anyway.

So, just nine days before Farrell announced his capitulation to Elstone, Ralph Hancox, the president of Reader's Digest Magazines Ltd., wrote me a letter in which he said that "for a variety of sound reasons...Reader's Digest in Canada consistently spells check as check as check [*sic*]". That seemed to me an uncommonly emphatic way to state an editorial policy that was then changed in little more than a week.

Elstone's exchange with the magazine was characterized by a greater measure of politeness than was mine. Referring to the wisecrack, Hancox wrote "This segment disturbs me on two counts: first, cultural chauvinism, particularly when it is applied to orthography, is a dangerous path for the unwary to follow. Second, your prejudicial jibe about Reader's Digest in Canada is not worthy of you". He passed along some well-researched material on the history of the word. This, while it might provide some argument in favour of the U.S. spelling, does not alter the fact that, to a literate Canadian, a cheque is a cheque is a cheque.

I replied (publicly) that my "prejudicial jibe" was just that, and while Hancox might have felt it was unworthy, he was in no position to say it was not worthy of me, because he did not know me. I don't know if he, or anyone else, was aware that I was just playing with words by then, but no matter. He also cited a number of statistics intended to demonstrate that many Canadians spend a lot of time reading his magazines and enjoy them very much, and I do not for a moment doubt that. It was not, however, a consideration that would deter me from making prejudicial jibes.

Farrell's last letter to Elstone extended "best wishes to a considerate and committed reader..." But in Elstone's last letter to me, that same "committed reader" went on at some length to explain that on the day in question he had been held up in a waiting room to the point at which "I had to read something. Anything."

Several readers of my first column on this subject pointed out that changing the spelling of anything in a direct quotation is an editorial sin, and that is true. However, Reader's Digest is primarily in the business of reprinting extracts and condensations of material from other publications, and the fact that Needham's quip was not displayed in quotation marks might give them an out. But surely they at least could have included some such parenthetical line as "(Translated from the Canadian)".

I thought the whole thing was fun, and it was evident that Mr. Elstone did, too, but that's only two out of three.

Another magazine that has a Canadian edition that annoys me is *Time*. I am a long-time subscriber. It somehow sticks in the back of my mind that I am buying an American magazine. That's what I want, but that's not what I get. I lived with that fact for a long time without complaining, but I was pushed to the brink a few years ago when the publication started converting every measurement to metric. I have learned to live with the half-assed implementation of the metric system that Pierre Trudeau dumped on us back in the 1970s, but I think it's insupportably condescending of *Time* to convert everything for me. The last thing I want to be told is that a basketball player is 213.36 cm tall. "Seven feet" will convey the information to me just fine. It doesn't bother me when a Canadian magazine uses metric, but *Time*'s knee-jerk conversion of every number in the book is infuriating and insulting. I have been to Denver, and recall its self-description as "The Mile-High City". I don't want to see it described *anywhere* as "The One-Point-Six-Zero-Nine-Three-Kilometre-High City", but that's exactly the kind of silliness the magazine's policy produces.

English-speaking Canadians, whether they are aware of it or not, are more sensitive to French than Americans. The way Americans pronounce French names and the many words and phrases borrowed from the French seems atrocious to many Canadians, who, while they might not speak the language, have had considerable experience of hearing it spoken. Listening to U.S. hockey commentators trying to cope with the many French names they are challenged with is good fun.

About French that has been englished: I do not say "onvelope" or "onvoy", but, come to think of it, I do say "on root". Some Americans say "on rowt" or "en root"; some even say "on root", but then will say "My son has a paper rowt". I have heard *route* pronounced "rowt" in the Canadian House of Commons, and that does bother me.

Wouldn't you think that in the 1990s, with the country teetering on the brink of a deadly schism, most CBC announcers would know that there are four, not five, syllables in *bilingualism*?

You used to be able to tell a Canadian from an American by the way each mispronounced *reveille*. I don't think this is so today. And — be honest — have you never said "lootenant" or "zee"? I have, and have been caught out by derisive acquaintances.

An American might "buy you a drink" in his own home, and we have picked up that one. But you would consider it quaint when an Englishman offers to "give you lunch" in a restaurant.

I've noticed that the more refined Americans pepper their speech with *you know*s, rather than *y'know*s, when what they really mean is *eh*.

The Canadian says "Nice day, eh?". The American says "Eh! Nice day!". I heard that from a comic on TV. Well, you have to *hear* it.

CHAPTER 9

Editors — Friends and Foes

Every writer needs a good editor. Bad writers need good editors, and good writers need them even more. A good editor can make a bad writer look good and a good writer look better. It's more important that a good writer have a good editor. A bad editor can make a bad writer look a little better, but can make a good writer look terrible. All writers make mistakes, but so do all editors. Bad editors miss real mistakes and correct non-existent ones. I should define what I mean by editors in the context of this chapter.

There are editors and there are editors. Look at the masthead of a newspaper or magazine and you will see a bewildering variety of titles that include the word. You may find editors-in-chief, managing editors, senior editors, junior editors, copy editors, photo editors, sports editors, executive editors, news editors, city editors, food editors, contributing editors, and God-knows-what-else editors.

The titles don't convey a great deal of information. A food editor does not edit food. He probably is someone who writes about restaurants and cookery and has been given an editor's title instead of a raise. A photo editor, obviously, is not required to have a mastery of the written word. A managing editor often is more manager than editor, although most of the ones I have known had been pretty good writers before they rose to that rank.

What I am talking about here is the editor who is supposed to be able to take a piece of writing and ensure that it is in English. Such editors are usually called copy editors, although their function may be performed by editors bearing other titles. They should not interfere with the writer's style unless the text is a straight news story and violates the established style of the publication or broadcasting organization. They are vital in a newsroom, because reporters pressed for time are primarily concerned with facts and often do not have time to fuss with style, or even spelling, but when there is time for careful writing there is time for thoughtful editing, and the former is not always accorded the latter.

Having worked both sides of the fence, I ought to say that I am wearing my writer's hat here, and that editors are going to get the worst of it. Were I editing, writers would not come off too well. That's the way it goes.

I am sure I am not alone in having had a career-long love-hate relationship with editors. I have greatly admired, and have been greatly helped by, some. And, then, there were the others.

Once I wrote a throwaway line in an article, to the effect that I prayed to be spared the ministrations of the kind of editor who would insert a comma between *Baja* and *California*. I had seen this done in a novel. The author was a friend of mine, and I was able to confirm that the error was not his. There was considerable response to what I wrote. I had calls and letters from people I knew and people I did not know. Most of them were writers or editors by trade. Some were perplexed; others were hostile. All made the point that surely it was standard practice to place a comma between the name of a town or city and the name of a state (or province, or country, or whatever). And, of course, they were right. Not a one, however, caught the point: there is no town in California named

Baja. *Baja California* is Spanish for what gringos call Lower California. It is that long finger of land that dangles along the west coast of
Mexico. None of those who reacted cottoned to that, even when I
pointed out that inserting the comma was tantamount to writing,
say, "Southern, Alberta" or "North, Dakota".

I have used that example more than once to support my argument that editors (and typesetters and proofreaders) should not be
allowed to change things without consulting the writer (by which I
really mean me; I don't care all that much about the others). That is
not an easy arrangement to achieve, but it is not impossible. I had
that understanding with a series of editors at *Books in Canada,* and
it was seldom violated. What made it possible was that I was able to
say tactfully that it was necessitated by the nature of the subject
matter and by the fact that I frequently made deliberate errors to
illustrate a point. Many times they would call me and ask if I *really*
meant to say that. As often as not I could say yes, but many times I
could only blush and thank them for sparing me a more public
embarrassment. There was an exception. My decades of newspaper
work had ingrained in me the unbreakable habit of writing *-or*
instead of the *-our* spelling favoured in Canadian publications
other than newspapers, and I welcomed having this weakness corrected automatically.

I have never, before or since, consistently had such a relationship with a publication, although I have had it with several individual editors. It can be born of mutual respect, which is the ideal, or,
in a seller's market, demanded by the writer. Once, when I was
wearing my editor's hat, Pierre Berton agreed to write a short piece
for me, on the condition that his paragraphing not be altered. I
understood his concern about paragraphing, which is approached
by most newspaper editors in an offhand manner that knows no
rule except the shorter the better, but I wondered if his very specific
proviso meant that he was giving me the option of messing up his

copy in other ways. I would not have dreamed of putting that possibility to the test.

A basic problem many reasonably experienced writers have is dealing with editors who, while they might be fairly competent at handling hard news stories according to the rules, don't understand that news writing is not the same as feature writing, and that writing a column is something else again. Over the years, I frequently have gone to bizarre lengths to bypass knee-jerk editors and get stuff into print exactly as I wrote it. That is living dangerously, but I'd rather risk having my own mistakes exposed than have my stuff butchered by someone who has no understanding of any style outside his stylebook and is death on literary devices. If there are to be mistakes, I prefer making my own to having someone else do it for me.

On newspapers and magazines, any writer who dares to complain about editorial tampering is regarded as a "prima donna" (I put that in quotes for a reason that should be obvious). Any bylined writer who doesn't, should — even at the risk of being labelled with a sexist pejorative. It is embarrassing enough, when something is published under your name, to have your style messed up, but it is downright humiliating to have your meaning altered or to have someone else's factual errors attributed to you, and it happens frequently. For a decade I have been trying to forget an incident in which all three of those indignities were inflicted on a very short magazine essay of mine. It was about 300 words in a painstakingly crafted parodic style. It fell into the hands of an editor newly hired from the copy desk of some newspaper in the boondocks. She attacked it with stylebook in one hand and blunt blue pencil in the other, and added some ideas and misinformation of her own, and to this day I can't think about it without squirming as agonizingly as I did the day I saw it in print under my name. I didn't get much satisfaction when I yelled about it, but the complaint wasn't entirely ineffectual. I was a regular contributor to that publication, and nothing quite that bad ever happened again.

I once wrote, in a commentary on the perils of electronic transmission of text, that a certain document that had undergone that process was "full of missing characters". I'd have fallen on my knees before an editor who had caught that gaffe. Where are they when you need them?

One of the first conventions taught to novice reporters when I was one was that of writing news stories in the "inverted pyramid" form, so that they could be chopped from the bottom up when space limitations demanded it. (I don't know if that is still taught. I don't know if *anything* is still taught.) Feature stories had a different structure (a beginning, a middle, and an end) because there was time for them to be edited carefully if cuts were required. I laboured for several years under a dim bulb of a city editor who never could grasp that concept (or, I sometimes thought, any other concept). It was only discussed once — I handed him a feature he thought was too long and I made the mistake of saying I had thought it might be, so had written it to be cuttable from the bottom, and he said "Oh, so you've finally learned how to do *that*, eh?", and I bit my tongue. I cannot recall one other editor I've worked *under* who didn't teach me something of value. He stands alone.

Stylebooks, even backed up by good dictionaries and reference works on grammar, can't do everything. An editor needs a good knowledge of English idiom, and I know of no way of acquiring that other than reading. There are reference works, of course, but there is a limit to the size of library one might expect a copy editor to have at his elbow. A dictionary may be helpful to an editor who learned English words by watching TV, but there isn't much help for him with idioms unless he's done some reading. I mention this here in passing, and refer you to Chapter 12 for some examples of what happens when people without a good grounding in the language absorb idiomatic English by ear only.

There has always, I guess, been a blur between the functions of editors and proofreaders. When I was starting, they had clearly defined mandates, but that is not to say the mandates were observed. The editor had the final say on the copy that was to be printed. The typesetter's job was to set the copy in type exactly as it was presented to him. The proofreader's job was to see that the typesetter had done *his* job. The proofreader had the original text, and would compare it with the galley proof of the typesetter's output.

Actually, though, it was not uncommon to find a proofreader who knew more about the rules and the publication's stylebook than did the editor. It was even more common to find proofreaders who *thought* they knew better. And it was not uncommon to find linotype operators who thought *they* knew better, and some of *them* did. So the "too many cooks" syndrome struck frequently.

With the arrival of computers in the newsroom, the number of slips 'twixt cup 'n' lip was reduced, but not eliminated. Today the editor is also the typesetter, and, for the most part, the proofreader (and, at some newspapers, also the compositor). There are still proofreaders, but their function is quite different. They still can and do mess things up occasionally, but the sharp eyes of the good ones are indispensable.

Once I walked into a meeting in the offices of a magazine with which I had a brief and tenuous editorial connection and found all the editors locked into a furious argument over whether an article referring to Mary Tyler Moore as "Mary" should be changed to adhere to the magazine's current policy, which would require calling her "Moore". At that time, the lady in question was at the top of the sitcom heap, venerated almost as widely as her two-millennium-old namesake, and to call her by her last name, without even so much as an honorific *Ms*, seemed close to sacrilege. I can't quite recall my advice as I headed out to the nearest bar, but, since we were talking television, its 1990s equivalent would be "Don't have a cow".

I don't have much patience with that degree of editorial pickiness. I wrote about television for the Toronto *Telegram* for a decade, during which I consistently flouted the house rule that dictated I must, in any piece in which I referred to the CBC, first identify it as the Canadian Broadcasting Corporation. I could accept the sense of that in general news stories (although I doubt that there is anyone in Canada who wouldn't know what *CBC* referred to), but considered it an entirely ridiculous constriction to place on entertainment-page columnists, who daily refer not only to the CBC, but to NBC, CBS, ABC, and the like. I am more interested in the fact that we conventionally refer to *the* CBC, but would never think of writing *the* CBS (or NBC or ABC), although each of those networks has a *the* preceding the full title. I assume we do this because the CBC is a national institution, like the Bell and the CPR. Is any of this worth having a cow about? I think not.

Headlines, for the most part, are written by editors. I remember an incident three or four decades ago, when *The Globe and Mail* was reporting on the annual report of the Canadian Broadcasting Corporation. There was nothing wrong with the story, but the headline said that the CBC had come out with a "deficit" of some hundreds of millions of dollars. There was no deficit. The amount cited was the amount by which the corporation's income fell short of the federal grant it received that year. To call that a deficit is either deceit or a reflection of incompetence. The headline sells the story, and as long as I've been around, some editors have been writing misleading headlines for just that purpose. They often display remarkable linguistic agility, but it's a disgusting, almost criminal, practice.

Many older writers and editors recommend studying W. Somerset Maugham's work as a model of a fine prose style, and I concur. I doubt that many young people do so today, but I read a lot of Maugham in my teens and twenties. I did not know until later that Maugham had an unofficial editor, in the person of Eddie Marsh, who was Winston Churchill's private secretary for many years. Marsh and Maugham were friends, perhaps more. Marsh was a brilliantly perceptive editor, and a merciless one, and Maugham acknowledged a great debt to him. Some of their correspondence has been published, revealing that Marsh contributed significantly to the elegance of Maugham's prose. It's well worth the while of any student of English to examine some of their letters.

Ernest Hemingway had a great and generally salubrious effect on twentieth-century literature. He laboured mightily at polishing his prose, but he also had Maxwell Perkins, who was his editor at Charles Scribner's Sons for many years. Perkins was a legend among editors. Among his other beneficiaries were F. Scott Fitzgerald, who simply could not spell, and Thomas Wolfe, whose glorious but undisciplined outpourings were like the finest of crude oil but needed to be processed by the Perkins refinery to keep your motor purring.

The literary world is not blessed with many such men. It never was, and probably never will be.

A chap in the television industry, whom I know fairly well, had a book published a few years ago. I was interested in reading it, but my pleasure was spoiled by tripping over dozens of errors in syntax. He was not primarily a print writer, and could have used a little editorial help. Apparently he did not get it, although the list of credits inside included one for editing.

There isn't much reason to expect things to get better, and that's as much your fault as anyone else's. There are economic realities in every business, and publishing is a business. Good editing is expensive. If people will uncomplainingly buy poorly edited books, they get what they deserve. The arts columnist Suanne Kelman, writing in *The Globe and Mail,* summed it up: "There's no payoff on sales for this kind of improvement...It is unjust to ask publishers to subsidize a purity that the market doesn't want and might not even recognize."

I have been told by acquaintances in that business that it simply is economically impossible for them to hire good editors, so I should just forget about it. What's more depressing is that I am told by acquaintances in the newspaper business that they *could* afford to hire good editors but can't find many.

There are some around, and there are others who would like to improve, but all, I think, are dispirited by the realization that it doesn't seem to matter much any more. Once I was asked by a newspaper executive to comment on the performance of an editor he was pleased to have hired. I said I could never feel quite comfortable with an editor who could not spell. "Oh", he said, "can't he spell?"

During the decade I was on staff at *The Telegram* in Toronto, I don't think there was a stylebook. I know someone was writing one during that time, but when the paper died in 1971 the opus still hadn't appeared. At one stage during that time, an edict came down from somewhere that, until we did get a stylebook, the arbiter in matters of style would be the then current *Gage* Canadian dictionary. Shortly after that, I filed a piece from out of town that contained a correct use of *parameters*. It appeared in print as *perimeters*. I was sufficiently annoyed to get on the phone and ask someone for an explanation. It seems that the editor who had handled my copy had looked up *parameter* in *Gage* and, failing to find it, assumed that I didn't know how to spell *perimeter*. Quite obviously, he didn't know how to read. He had interpreted the edict about style to mean that anything that wasn't in the skimpy little *Gage* wasn't a word.

An editor once told me, in a telephone conversation, "My wife conv— oops...persuaded me I was wrong". Interesting. He knew, and cared, that there is a distinction between *persuade* and *convince,* but was not pleased to be told he had it backward. I once phoned an editor to tell him I had been rechecking a story I had sent him and noticed I had mistakenly used a *which* instead of a *that.* He said he had already fixed it. I thanked him and congratulated him on his sharp eye, whereupon he informed me that he *always* changed *which*es to *that*s.

Here is one of my favourite slaps at editors. The essayist B.W. Powe wrote a piece for *The Globe and Mail* about what he called "post-literacy". He began by quoting a telephone call he had received from an editor who had been working on an article by Powe.

"I've corrected the typos in the manuscript", the editor told him, "including the one in your name. You left the two Ls off Powell."

Indignant, Powe answered: "Do you think I'd misspell my own name?"

"Well, how was I supposed to know?" the editor said. "You spelled Hemingway with only one M."

Powe swore that this was a true story, but I wouldn't have doubted it for a moment. I have long since lost count of the number of times I've seen would-be writers express their admiration of

"Hemmingway". It turned my thoughts back forty years, to my first newspaper job. The paper had hired a reporter whom the editors judged to be incompetent but for some reason did not wish to fire. The solution was an appointment as copy editor. I thought it bizarre at the time, but I found out the hard way that it is not so uncommon.

CHAPTER 10

"But It's in the Dictionary..."

I have a lot of dictionaries around the house. I've tried to count them, but always distract myself by picking one up and starting to browse. I know there are more than fifty. Some of them are paperbacks or pocket editions; some I can't lift with one hand. Some are narrowly specialized, dealing with technical terms or foreign languages. I think this is more than you would find in the average household. I think so because so many people, when their use of a word is challenged, will say that they "looked it up in the dictionary".

"*The* dictionary." I've heard that phrase all my life, and I still have to bite my tongue to avoid using it myself. There are, I surmise, thousands of different dictionaries, some of which fall much farther short of perfection than others. One can consult *a* dictionary, but not *the* dictionary. Most families would have one dictionary in the house, and that would be *the* dictionary, but only to them.

If you settle on one dictionary that you're going to adopt as your standard reference, it's a good idea to read some of that fine print in the front of the book (the part in which the pages are numbered in roman numerals). It will give you some warning signs of what is untrustworthy about that particular one. For example, when a word has more than one definition, some dictionaries will list the most firmly established meaning first, while others will give first place to the newest meaning. Or there may be some other standard for ordering definitions. It can be important to know this.

I keep two *big* and expensive U.S. dictionaries lying open on racks beside my desk. My personal attitude is that one (almost a half-century old) is to tell me what words mean, and the other (published in 1987) is to tell me what too many people *think* they mean. The old one is *Webster's New International Dictionary, Second Edition, Unabridged,* and the new one is *The Random House Dictionary of the English Language, Second Edition, Unabridged.* The *Webster* was *the* dictionary in one of the first newspaper offices I worked in, and that no doubt accounts in part for my bias toward it. I will have no truck whatsoever with the non-prescriptive *Webster* third edition, which I regard merely as a chronicle of everything that has gone wrong with the language. Another modern one, used by many U.S. writers, is *The American Heritage Dictionary,* which I do not have. I can't buy *all* of them. A late friend and colleague used to cite the *American Heritage* in defence when I would charge him with faulty usage, so I think that tells me something about that one.

While this book was in preparation, the long-awaited new edition of the *OED* came out. Its cost is far beyond my means. When I cite the *OED* in these pages, I am referring to the one that has been kicking around almost as long as I have. The only reason I have that one at my disposal is that it is available in a physically compressed form at a bargain price. For those who have not seen them, I should explain that the compact *OED* editions utilize an optical reduction technique that enables the printing of four pages of the original on each page of these cumbersome volumes, which are best studied with the aid of a magnifying glass. The two main volumes and the new supplement comprise more than 20,000 pages, and, since I can afford neither the money nor the shelf space to have the real thing on hand, I am grateful for this publishing gimmick, however awkward it may be to use.

Dictionaries (and the lexicographers behind them) fall loosely into two classes: prescriptive and descriptive, although there is a lot of overlap. Everyone should have at least one of each (dictionary, that is, not lexicographer), but if I could have only one, I would choose a prescriptive one, and they are getting hard to find. My big *Webster* is prescriptive. Its sorry successor is descriptive.

I utterly fail to see why these divisions are necessary. Most of us turn to a dictionary primarily to find out what is *right*. The descriptivists (and the ones whose blather I have read are a truly tedious bunch of oafs) argue that nothing is "right"; that their job is simply to record the way the language is being used (or, I would add, misused). Well, I surely do appreciate having such a record, but it's not enough. There should be dictionaries that will tell you first what, in their opinion, is correct, and *then* tell you about all those widespread misuses.

The *RH-II* is not too bad. It doesn't approach the *Webster* in heft, and it contains only about half as many words, but its editors have been alert to neologisms and have not entirely abandoned the concept of being at least a tad prescriptive. Some reviews I had read before it arrived had suggested that it was grossly permissive, although none was as splenetic as Dwight McDonald's classic diatribe in *The New Yorker* when the third edition of *Webster* came out.

The new edition was a welcome addition to my collection, being (for a time, at least) the newest big, serious dictionary around. It was the first new entry in its class since 1966, when *RH-I* was published, and boasts "over 315,000 entries in 2500 pages" and "over 50,000 new words and 75,000 new meanings". (I am quoting here from the dust jacket, and if you are put off by the missing comma or the misuse of *over*, please do not judge the book by its cover.) It weighs in at a respectable 10.5 pounds on my kitchen scales, but is a slender volume in comparison with the *Webster* second (600,000 entries in 3,200 pages and too heavy for said scales). Its type is easier on tired old eyes. Alas, it skimps on etymology.

The first word I looked for, of course, was *hopefully*. Although what I found put me in a snit, it also introduced me to a welcome feature: "usage" notes appended to many controversial definitions. Here, again, is the usage note on *hopefully*.

> Although some strongly object to its use as a sentence modifier, HOPEFULLY meaning "it is hoped (that)" has been in use since the 1930's and is fully standard in all varieties of speech and writing: *Hopefully, tensions between the two nations will ease.* This use of HOPEFULLY is parallel to that of *certainly, curiously, frankly, regrettably*, and other sentence modifiers.

Setting aside the fact that I have dug in my heels for life on the matter of *hopefully*, I was discouraged by a couple of other things in that paragraph: the use of *ease* as an intransitive verb and the apostrophe in *1930's*, not to mention the manner in which the writer is begging the question by saying that the use is parallel to the other four adverbs he lists. But there is something almost puckish about the whole thing, and I decided not to heave the book out the window just yet. Instead, I turned to the new supplement to the *OED* (which had come in the mail the same day) and found an added meaning for *hopefully*:

> It is hoped (that); let us hope. (Cf. G. *hoffentlich* it is to be hoped.) orig. *U.S.* (Avoided by many writers.)

As everyone knows, the *OED* is basically an historical dictionary. When it prescribes, it does so with British restraint. If it says that a use is avoided by *many* writers, it obviously means *good* writers, although it is too polite to come right out and say that. Something else I appreciate in the *OED* is its use of *properly.* When that word precedes a definition, you know that there are other definitions coming that merely describe recorded misuses of the word.

I would not characterize *RH-II* as a prescriptive dictionary, but it is a tad closer to being one than is the rigorously descriptive *Webster* third. For instance, it admits, however reluctantly, that it might be worthwhile to preserve the distinction between *imply* and *infer.* I thought that was damn' decent of its editors.

One of the many entries that annoyed me was the one for *rhetoric,* which seems to have become a pejorative while I wasn't looking. In other times, we used to speak of "hollow rhetoric" or "empty rhetoric", but *rhetoric* per se was merely an instrument to be used by a talented writer or speaker, who, were he a demagogue, might put rhetoric to evil use. We might say his speech was *merely* rhetoric. But we might also say approvingly of some worthy politician that his speech made good use of rhetoric. Now we have "the dictionary" making a dirty word of it.

Perhaps *rhetoric* is now a lost cause. As I pointed out in Chapter 2, exactly the same thing is in the process of happening to *graphic* and *explicit.* The dismal clods in newsrooms everywhere who are turning these into dirty words ought to be called to account by irate readers and viewers before they catch the attention of the descriptivist lexicographers who are so anxious to turn the English-speaking world into a tower of babble.

While making notes for this book, I more than once jotted down *moot.* I was noticing more and more instances of its being used to mean (judging by the context) pointless to discuss, not worth talking about. As far as I was concerned, it meant arguable or open to debate or not proven. After consulting a few dictionaries, I found my interpretation was still right, but was being overtaken by what I considered to be the misuse. The upshot was that I decided I should stop using the word at all while I was still ahead. One more release of a major new dictionary and it's dead.

I am fond of quoting Lewis Carroll's line: "'When I use a word,' Humpty Dumpty said, 'it means just what I choose it to mean — neither more nor less.'" The descriptivists are bent on legitimatizing all the Humpty Dumptys of the world.

One day a couple of decades ago, when I was involved in a brief and ill-advised foray into television production, I glanced at the output of a character generator, the device that creates and stores those lines of type that appear on the bottom of your TV screen to identify the talking heads that appear above them. This one identified a speaker as a "restauranteur". I told the operator to change it to *restaurateur*. He gave me an argument, and I told him he could check it himself if he wanted to, and *then* make the change. The program went on the air without the correction. When I challenged the culprit he said he had checked, and I was wrong. He handed me a tattered old *Webster's Collegiate* (a respectable enough reference for its scope). I looked, and pointed out that the word was not even there, and he said it was, and pointed to the entry for *restaurant* and explained that one simply had to add *-eur*. "I *knew* it had an N", he crowed. The truth is that anyone who looks into the etymology of *restaurant* (which is quite interesting) will see immediately why there is no N in *restaurateur,* and might even remember to get it right henceforth. Newer dictionaries, recognizing the commonness of the mistake, allow it as an alternative spelling.

The young man, who was bright in many respects, aspired to be a writer. He told me once that he didn't pay much attention to spelling, because "that's what editors are for". I don't know what became of him, but it wouldn't surprise me to learn he had realized his ambition, not because there were editors around to help him, but because many publications nowadays apparently don't care a fig about spelling. He probably continues to consult dictionaries the way many people do, seeing only what he wants to see. What he wants to see is validation of his own misconceptions. He will find that in many newer dictionaries, and will not go past that to note that the better among the newer ones will recommend that the common misuse be eschewed.

I have met the actor Patrick Macnee, and found him to be an articulate and engaging conversationalist. I can't imagine his not knowing that the word is *restaurateur*, not "restauranteur", yet he coolly and deliberately and clearly used the latter in a TV commercial. I hope he was paid a great deal of money for committing this atrocity.

Books of synonyms sell well. They have their uses, but they are no substitute for a good dictionary. It is becoming common to misuse *notorious* in place of *infamous*. A casual look at a book of synonyms, even the revered *Roget's Thesaurus* (which takes more care than most with subtle distinctions), might lead one to believe that the two words are interchangeable, and evidently a lot of writers do believe that. Were they to consult a good dictionary, they would learn that *infamous* is invariably deprecatory, while *notorious* is not necessarily so. *Notorious* basically means well-known, according to the *OED*, which also defines *infamous* as meaning notorious *for* badness of any kind. While it would be correct to describe someone as being notorious for his philanthropy, it might be inadvisable to do so today; however, a notorious philanderer is not quite the same thing as an infamous one. There is still a distinction worth preserving here.

A distinction evidently not worth preserving, in the minds of

some lexicographers, is that between *depreciatory* and *deprecatory.* I
used *depreciatory* in the previous paragraph, and then started to
think about it. A quick look at the desk dictionary inside my computer told me I could have used either. A look at my *Webster* told me
I had chosen correctly. A look at the *RH-II* told me I should have
used *deprecatory,* and since I was feeling modern at the moment, I
changed it. This is a truly stupid state of affairs.

Someone wrote me to object to the use of *characterize* for
describe, suggesting that it gained currency during the Watergate
hearings and has become beloved of inquisitorial legislators.
Sources say (hell, why should I go on typing in the names of reference books when I can just say *sources say*, as the newspersons do?)
that *characterize,* in one of its senses, means describe or delineate
the character or peculiar qualities of a person or thing. I think that
to ask someone to characterize someone is to ask for something
more than a mere description, and that the context will indicate
whether the word is being used appropriately or pretentiously.

Many such distinctions are becoming increasingly blurred, or
lost outright — if they ever existed at all. I have always valued the
distinction between *imply* and *infer.* Should you choose to disagree
with me, you can find ample support in the *OED*; however, my
Webster offers this under *infer*: "5. Loosely and erroneously, to
imply." The implication here — or such is my inference — is that
some lexicographers felt this distinction to be useful and attempted
to encourage it. I'm with them.

In his review of *RH-II* for *Time,* Christopher Porterfield notes an
entry for "kudo", and asks "What next? Will a single instance of
pathos be called a patho?".

Mere words cannot describe the depth of the depression into which
I was plunged one day by the receipt of a letter from A.A. Cameron,

the chief librarian of the Georgina Public Library in Keswick, Ontario, who wrote: "I was appalled to learn that you consult Webster's dictionary, and even confess it...Webster's is the catechism of Babel and should be found in the office only if your desk has a short leg."

My chagrin arises from the realization that A.A. Cameron (nowadays one dare not make assumptions about the gender of a correspondent who signs himself or herself thus, so the use of a pronoun here is ruled out) had jumped to the conclusion that when I say *Webster* I am referring to the infamous third edition, for which A.A. Cameron's loathing cannot possibly exceed my own. I was quick to reply that the *Webster* of my formative years was the unabridged second edition, for which I retain a high regard. The publication of the third edition is an event I have tried to wipe from my memory, and I was shattered to learn that A.A. Cameron could believe I would have any truck with a dictionary that countenances the use of *infer* for *imply.*

One should be able to trust those who devise crossword puzzles to be uncommonly painstaking in their use of words. It was, therefore, most distressing to note in a recent, usually respectable, syndicated puzzle the use of *imply* as a definition for *infer*, thereby undermining the work of generations of educators who have gone grey (or, in some cases, gray) trying to preserve the distinction by telling students "I imply; you infer". The inference to be drawn is that the puzzle-maker was using an inferior dictionary. The distinction is not difficult to grasp, and it is a useful and important one, but the misuse of *infer* for *imply* (which for some reason is more common than the reverse) has become so widespread that some dictionaries have given up on it and simply list the latter as a synonym for the former, without comment. If you have such a dictionary, replace it.

"[He] finds it humorous that he, the son of a Jewish manufacturer from Montreal, and yours truly, the son of a Newfoundland fisherman, hobnob with the hoi polloi."

That paragraph appeared in "Canada's national newspaper" under the byline of one of its most prestigious (I use the word advisedly) critics and feature writers.

Here we have no mere typographical error. Here we have a writer using a phrase whose meaning he doesn't know. The context makes it clear that he was looking for some such term as *upper crust,* or *elite,* or *crème de la crème,* and he made a compound boo-boo.

Hoi polloi is Greek. It means, literally, the many. It is used properly to refer to the masses, the man in the street, the common folk, and so on.

It's unfortunate that the phrase crept into English use, or, rather, misuse. The *OED* itself ignores it, although the phrase finds a place in the supplement that it should have found in the original. The first citation is from Dryden's *Essay of Dramatic Poesy* (1668), and it is an ominous one: "If by the people you understand the multitude, the *hoi polloi,* 'tis no matter what they think; They are sometimes in the right, sometimes in the wrong; their judgement is a mere lottery."

Well, that, I guess, is where the trouble started. Dryden used the redundant *the* before *hoi,* which means the, and other English writers of note followed his lead.

I think we're stuck with the redundancy. If, in formal writing, you were to insert the phrase in Greek characters, doubtless it would go down well, but if, in informal writing or conversation, you were to use the phrase without the *the,* you would get funny looks.

However, Fowler refused to buy the pleonasm. "The best solution", he wrote, "is to eschew the phrase altogether, but it is unlikely to be forgotten as long as *Iolanthe* is played: *'Twill fill with joy and madness stark the Hoi polloi (a Greek remark)."*

While I don't believe there's much point in being stuffy about the *the*, I can't buy the attitude affected on this (or any) subject by Jim Quinn in his little book, *American Tongue and Cheek*, wherein, with more commercial acumen than serious purpose, he attempts to pander to *hoi polloi* by telling them they can't be faulted for calling themselves "the" *hoi polloi*, and by declaring that such "word snobs" as Fowler and William Safire are really word *slobs*, and it's okay to speak lousy. Quinn is clever and amusing, but he draws heavily on the *OED* when it suits his purpose and fails to remind us that it is an historical dictionary and that its every citation is not to be taken as an example of desirable usage.

The fact that Dryden, Byron, and Cooper, *inter alios*, used the superfluous *the* does not make it right any more than the fact that a president of the United States, poor, ailing, thick-tongued Ike Eisenhower, couldn't pronounce *nuclear* makes it right for today's generation of thick-skulled TV newsmen to go on pronouncing it "nucular". Anyway, the point of all this is not that the author of the wrong use of *hoi polloi* quoted above used a redundant *the*. The point is that he (and, God knows, he is not alone in his culpability) misused the term in an attempt to convey the opposite of what it means. It troubles me that every authority I've referred to about *hoi polloi* really has nothing to say about it save to deplore or forgive the egregious extra *the*. None has mentioned the fact that it is becoming commonly misused by writers who should know better.

Surely there's nothing wrong with getting terribly upset when a commonly respected essayist misuses a phrase so grotesquely. This was not a matter of nuance. The man was saying black when he meant white; yes when he meant no; right when he meant wrong. He did not invent the mistake. Possibly it arises because of confusion with the term *hoity-toity*, which itself seems to have evolved in some confusion. To most of us today, it connotes haughtiness or arrogance, but its first meaning is related to its origin in the verb *hoit*, which means to indulge in noisy mirth.

It's not hard to imagine some people associating *hoity-toity* with *high-and-mighty*, and the *OED* draws our attention to the variation, *highty-tighty*. Perhaps the syllable *hoi* is enough, in some minds, to evoke an image of hoity-toitiness.

At least this is something we can look up. Twice in the last few days I've been confused by writers who referred to a man as a *bimbo*. I know *bimbo* is a kind of brandy punch, and I know that in Mexico it's the brand name for a local equivalent of our plastic sliced bread. When I was a boy, it was a sexist slang word interchangeable with *broad*. To learn what it meant in what to me was a strange context, I had to consult an editor considerably younger than I, who informed me, in a rather hoity-toity manner, that, to *hoi polloi* of today a bimbo is a nerd.

While I'm often critical of dictionaries, they are invaluable when used intelligently, and it's distressing that so many writers today use them only to justify sloppy writing. A sharp-eyed reader once rapped me for writing "his chair *sits* vacant", when I should have used *stands*. It took me one minute to find support (from *Webster*) for my use of *sits* in that context and shut him up. We all do it. But in my heart I wished I had written *stands*.

The fact that a dictionary may say that a word is sometimes spelled a certain way doesn't mean that it is an acceptable alternative spelling. Nor does the mention that a word has been seen or heard to be used in a certain way justify *your* using it that way. There are some good dictionaries and a lot of bad dictionaries. Sloppy writers love the bad ones, for obvious reasons.

Minuscule is so often misspelled that many modern dictionaries condone the spelling "miniscule", which masks the etymology.

I once had to ask publicly for help with *maven,* a current pet of yuppie journalists. I looked for it for some time before finding it first in Arthur Naiman's *Every Goy's Guide to Common Jewish Expressions* and later in a couple of quite recent and rather inadequate U.S. dictionaries. All I found was that it means expert, and I wondered if we really need another word for that, or if it had some further connotation that I hadn't found.

Marcia Tannenbaum, of Ottawa, sent me a welcome response:

> A maven is not simply an expert, one who knows a lot about a particular area of knowledge but also, more importantly, *one who understands...*The word comes from the Hebrew verb "to understand", *l'haveen...*I trust that this is sufficient information to persuade [*sic*] you that the language is indeed enriched by [the use of the] word, *maven.*

I guess that provides some justification. I have always felt that *expert* bore some connotation of understanding, and, in fact, *understanding,* in one of its senses, means expert. However, *understanding* has a broader meaning, and, from what Ms Tannenbaum says, I am willing to concede that there is value in having a noun such as *maven* in English. It certainly beats *understander.*

For most of my life, I believed that a fact was something that is true. I was brought up to believe that, and was in my sixties before the thought occurred to me to look it up in a dictionary — and then another dictionary, and then another...

At first I couldn't understand how all of them could be wrong; then I put on my Humpty Dumpty hat and decided that they *were* wrong, and I am sticking by that. A fact is a fact is a fact, and that's a fact. Let the dictionaries catch up with me.

If I tell you "...and that's a fact", you can say "no it isn't", and we

can argue. You can say that I am presenting as fact some information that is not true, but I won't let you get away with saying my
facts are wrong. By my definition, a fact cannot be wrong — if it is
wrong, then it is not a fact — but *I* can be wrong in saying something is a fact when, in fact, it isn't. The lexicographers may quibble
as they will, but the people have spoken: the fact remains that
unless *fact* is understood to be something that is true, the word
becomes almost useless.

RH-II says *factoid* is a word. It means "something suspicious or
unsubstantiated that is presented as fact...". Now, c'mon, *RH-II,* if a
fact is not necessarily true, what is wrong with presenting something suspicious or unsubstantiated as a fact? If a fact is not a fact,
how did we come to get the word *factoid*?

The fact is that many dictionaries are full of references to *fact* in
which they treat the word as meaning something that is true, but
then they waffle when it comes to actually defining the word.

I can't say too often that there is a lot of highfalutin crap spouted
by lexicographers, many of whom are otherwise deserving of great
respect in many respects, about what a dictionary should be. They
lose sight of what most people *want* a dictionary to be: a guide to
good usage.

It should take more than widespread misuse by a lot of sloppy
writers and talkers to justify any dictionary's condoning it.

The Globe and Mail published a letter from Thomas M. Paikeday, chief editor of Winston Dictionaries of Canadian English,
challenging an assertion by Robertson Davies that *momentarily*
means fleetingly or for a moment, and does not mean anything like
very soon or at any moment now.

In his attempted refutation, Mr. Paikeday cites three dictionaries (none of them his; he is gallant about this), all published since
1976. A fig for them! The only one of the three that I might pay
attention to is the 1976 supplement to the *OED,* which, he says,
"confirms the disputed sense of *at any moment* with citations

dating from 1928 to 1975". That, in itself, means nothing. The *OED,* being an historical dictionary, is awash with citations, dating from the dawn of recorded history, that prove nothing except that modern writers have no corner on the misuse of words. Unlike some of its upstart counterparts, the *OED* usually has the good grace to indicate the undesirability of imitating such abuses. Furthermore, one of the younger dictionaries on my shelf is the *Oxford American Dictionary* (1980), and it offers only one definition — the correct one — of *momentarily.*

One doesn't even *need* a dictionary for this word, which is the adverbial form of *momentary.* People don't misuse or misunderstand *momentary*; why should they have a problem with *momentarily*?

Mr. Paikeday refers to a history of *momentarily,* in the sense of at any moment, starting less than sixty years ago. That is such a short time in the history of language that it might indicate that this is but a momentary aberration; however, there is little doubt that it will be carefully nurtured by modern lexicographers, who, in their righteous zeal to keep up with things, tend to forget that it is possible to be descriptive without abandoning their responsibility to be prescriptive as well.

It may be that there is already a dictionary (and, if there is not, bet the farm that there will be) that says of the word *nuclear* "often pronounced *nucular*", and hundreds of inept newscasters will stand up to cheer and shout in chorus: "See! I was right all along."

CHAPTER 11

Taboos

Nowadays it is permissible to print all the old favourite unprintable words, including the F-word, the C-word, and even the M-word. You can also say them in the movies and on pay-TV, and, most marvellous of all, in 1991 it became permissible (and, for a short while, almost mandatory, it seemed) to say *piss* on U.S. network television.

But...don't ever dare to call a woman a lady! That's now a four-letter word in the classic sense.

I wonder why it is possible to arouse mobs to viciously enforce "politically correct" language while it remains virtually impossible to get many folk even mildly interested in grammatically correct language.

Of all the sins against ear or eye, the one that sets my dentures on edge above the others is the use of *they* as a third-person singular pronoun. I was quite pleased a few decades ago when the feminist movement came up with a new honorific for women who do not wish to disclose their marital status. I refer to *Ms*, a useful neologism that quickly found wide acceptance. (The only problem with it is that people tend to put a period after it, as they do with *Mr.* and *Mrs.* These are abbreviations [of *Master* and *Mistress*], and so require the period. *Ms* is not an abbreviation of anything, so does not require a period any more than does *Miss.* There are dictionaries that disagree with me on this. If they argue that the term was coined with the period attached, I say the coiner was wrong. Period.) I wish the same movement had come up with a neutral singular third-person pronoun at the same time. There have been attempts, but none has caught on.

The misuse of the plural pronoun is, of course, the result of people leaning over backward to avoid slighting women. I have no quarrel with that motive, but I suggest that it isn't necessary to lean as far as everyone seems to think to achieve the objective. I was part of what was perhaps the last generation of students to be educated (and reporters to be trained) to adhere to the centuries-old convention of using the masculine third-person singular pronoun unless the antecedent was clearly feminine. The practice grew deep roots, and while I was game to try to adapt to the new order, I have frequently caught myself backsliding, particularly in conversation.

On the other hand, I don't believe I have ever written *they* or *them* or *their* in place of a singular pronoun. It's something that grates horribly on my sensibilities whenever I read or hear it, and these days that is every few minutes. I'm quite serious about that — it has, for me, the quality of a fingernail on a slate. What intensifies my irritation is that the practice is virtually unnecessary.

There is more than one way to skin a cat. To the writer who nervously chooses to pen such abominations as "If a person wants to do something badly, they will find a way", I suggest that anyone who wants to do something *well* will find a way. (This might be as good a place as any to point out something that shouldn't need to be pointed out: to say "I want to do this badly" is not the same as saying "I badly want to do this", or even "I want badly to do this". It is a good idea to stay away from *badly* altogether if you can't put it in the right position. If you replace *badly* with *very much*, it won't matter as much where you place it, but you will run afoul of the many teachers who insist that you should eschew *very*.)

There are many other ways around the problem, and I am *not* talking about resorting to *his-or-her* or *he/she* or anything like that, although I prefer that approach (as a last resort) to the plural pronoun with the singular antecedent. For the past couple of years, I have been stumbling over a TV commercial for a product that claims to improve the learning skills of students. I have come close to injuring myself grabbing for the remote control to switch channels. The key line I am trying to avoid is so offensive to me that (I have just realized) I have neither memorized it nor written it down, but it goes something like this: "The most important contribution you can make to your child's future is their education." This would bother me even if the product being pitched were acne cream, and the fact that it is supposed to be educational material makes it ten times as bad.

What would be wrong, for example, with changing "their education" to "a good education"? It would be an improvement, actually, because it is possible to contribute a *bad* education to your children — by exposing them to stupid TV commercials, for example. There are many other options.

As if this weren't enough, this gender sensitivity has gone to the ridiculous extreme of producing sentences such as "Any person is entitled to have an abortion if they want one". Have I missed something? Are men having abortions now? (Perhaps they are. I spotted a reference on a Toronto TV station to a "female maternity clinic", and I suppose this distinction was made to ensure that no one would assume it was one of those male maternity clinics.) You can see what's been going on here. Once the misuse of *they* became politically correct, the door was open to a whole fresh flood of sloppiness. Time and again today you will see the plural pronoun being used when there is no doubt at all of the gender of the antecedent. The proper pronoun in the quotation above would be *she*. (I am resisting the temptation to digress here and ask if a better construction would be "if they wants one", but it seems to me to be a question that ought to be dealt with.) A computer consultant, writing about the controversy over whether computers should be left running or turned off when temporarily not in use (trust me — leave 'em on), wrote: "One of my clients has gone two years without turning their machine off." In this case, surely he knows whether his client is male or female. His sort inevitably will replace the singular with the plural pronoun all the time. We will hear nothing but such abominations as "My mother always brings home work from their office" and "My brother won't let me borrow their bicycle".

Here's another one, from a talk show dealing with the 1991 bestseller *Final Exit*. They (this *they* being the hostess, of course) introduced the topic with this question: "Should an individual have the right to take his or her own life if they are facing a terminal illness?"

Not surprisingly, this mess has come into being in a most disorderly fashion. I have not been able to get any supporter of this nonsense to tell me if I should say "This is a decision a person must make for themself". That would seem to make more sense than saying "themselves", since *them* is being treated as singular. The people who started all this gave no thought to the morrow. Another commercial tells us that "everyone has their own reason" for something or other. Shouldn't that be "everyone *have* their own reason"?

Even today, it is argued by many scholars, writers, and editors (of all sexes) that English does not need a new pronoun that means either he or she; it already has one, and that pronoun is *he*. I find the habit hard to break, and I may have inadvertently followed that old rule from time to time in this book. I thought about making some corrections, but decided not to. These lapses serve as a reminder of times when life was a lot simpler for writers, and, to me, adherence to the old rule provided prose that was a lot cleaner than that produced by the use of plural pronouns with singular antecedents. Also, it's my goddam book.

When Thurgood Marshall was retiring from the United States Supreme Court, he jumped on a reporter at a press conference for using the term *black people*. "I am not a black people", he said, "I am an African-American." I can remember (although I am growing confused) when *Negro* was politically correct, when *coloured* was politically correct, when *black* was politically correct, and perhaps more that I don't remember. Much of this was before the term *politically correct* came into use, but the concept existed. All this is okay with me, but it makes me nervous, and I would like to be pardoned for sometimes failing to keep up. I am not particularly concerned with being politically correct, but I am concerned with being respectful of others. More recently, I was listening to a televised conversation between Jesse Jackson and Spike Lee. In that half-hour the term *black people* was spoken dozens of times, but I heard *African-American* only once or twice. Is it not reasonable to take a cue from them?

On the other hand, it imposes a considerable strain on people to remember that many common and long-entrenched idiomatic expressions in English might be deemed offensive as long as *black* remains the designation of a race. It seems to me it was only yesterday that one could speak confidently of *black humour* when referring to a foul mood. Today it could refer to an Eddie Murphy joke. It does get to be a handful. Here is a correction that appeared in a California newspaper:

> An item in Thursday's Nation Digest about the Massachusetts budget crisis made reference to new taxes that will help put Massachusetts "back in the African-American." The item should have said "back in the black".

I suppose a computer (or perhaps an editor) had been programmed to make politically correct changes, and the programmer
had forgotten that *black* has more than one connotation. Would the
same program have spewed out the information that until the taxes
do their work, Massachusetts will remain in the indigenous people?
I can imagine similar problems if one set out to avoid the sin, mentioned above, of calling a woman a lady. A drama critic might pick
up the paper some day and find his review of *The Importance of
Being Earnest* making references to the actress who played Woman
Bracknell. How does *The Woman of Shalott* grab you? Or *Woman
Chatterley's Lover*?

Probably no one would ever be accused of insensitivity for
using *holocaust* in its basic sense, but I feel nervous whenever I do
so. It has been pretty well pre-empted for the purpose of evoking
the horrors of the genocide perpetrated by the Nazis in the 1930s
and '40s, and it now seems almost disrespectful to use it in relation
to anything less horrendous. It is quite correct to describe the fire-
bombing of Dresden in World War II as a holocaust, but sometimes
I might be inclined to look for another word.

I mourn the loss of the word *gay*. It was a happy, light-hearted
word. You don't often see a word change that quickly. Many words
are in the process of becoming useless, but this one went almost
overnight. Now it means homosexual and nothing else. You can no
longer speak of a time when hearts were young and gay, or say you
were having a gay old time, or refer to the Gay Nineties without
seriously confusing people, but you can talk about gay rights or
gay-bashing and be easily understood.

You don't need a very long memory to recall when one didn't
discuss homosexuality in polite circles. The change in this situation
has had some bizarre effects on our language. We have seen the
emergence of *homophobia,* a word that surely ought to mean fear of

either men or monotony, but it appears to mean fear of homosexuals, and is so defined in *RH-II*. It used to be common enough to drop into the neighbourhood store and ask for a quart of homo milk. I would think twice before doing that today, especially in the neighbourhood I lived in twenty years ago, which has undergone some demographic changes. I have written in these pages of homophones and homonyms with some degree of nervousness.

I wish there had been more thought given to labelling the acquired immuno-deficiency syndrome as AIDS. It raises a couple of problems. Audio-visual aids became commonplace in our schools in my time. I don't know if that term is still in use, but it could cause some confusion. It's a well-known fact that the prime minister has aides, and it's okay to put that in print. I would hesitate to write it in a newscast script.

Since I retain fond memories of one great English teacher I had fifty years ago, I can't use the phrase "schoolteachers' superstitions" without feeling a twinge of guilt for my ingratitude, but then I remember all the other teachers, ranging from indifferent to bad, and I go ahead and use it anyway. It refers to many of the convenient rules we all were ordered to take to heart for life, no matter how oversimplified they were.

I have a long-time friend about my age who, while he is not a professional writer, has to do a tremendous amount of writing. He was fortunate to have had one very good teacher of English while he was in high school, and he was a good student. When he writes, he follows the rules she taught him, and he writes well, but he and I argue over what I call his slavish adherence to her teachings. I try to make the point that he will always be well served by following her precepts when he is writing, but not necessarily when he is reading. He tends to judge others by the extent to which they follow the basic rules he was taught, and English is not that simple.

People have often taken me to task for splitting infinitives. I do it, and will go on doing it. Most authorities are reasonably flexible on the subject. As a general rule, the split infinitive should be avoided, but not beyond the point at which the avoidance causes awkwardness of expression. To put it another way, if you split an infinitive to conveniently avoid awkwardness of expression, you'll get no flak from me. I am not interested in perpetuating school-teachers' bugbears. I do want to encourage users of English to try to say what they mean.

Children of my generation had another rule drummed into us, one which, out of sheer perversity, I choose to remember today as "Prepositions are not for ending sentences with". There is a famous line on this subject attributed to Sir Winston Churchill: "It is a practice up with which I cannot put." It's a lost cause, Teach, because it never should have been a rule in the first place.

CHAPTER 12

Confusibles

Some time ago, I was trying out a new piece of computer software (not "softwear", as it is spelled by a surprising number of people who should know better but who possibly are obsessed with having comfortable undergarments), and it reported on the screen that it was altering my instructions slightly, "do to" something. Since the context was a line of technical jargon and abbreviations, I didn't realize instantly what was meant. Then it dawned on me that the programmer was using it as in "do to circumstances beyond our control". Now, that does not look like an obvious typo, yet I couldn't quite believe that he was unable to spell *due*. Subsequently, I noticed the error in many other places, and remembered that *due* is pronounced that way in many parts of the United States. More recently, I've seen the mistake being made by Canadians. I guess that's inevitable.

One way or another, often because of similarities in spelling or pronunciation, there are pairs or even groups of words that mix people up. There are many books devoted entirely to this subject, such as *Room's Dictionary of Confusibles* and James Kilpatrick's *The Ear Is Human*. Our professional writers and speakers seem not to read such books. Some evidence for that statement is presented in this chapter. I am not trying to compete with Room or Kilpatrick or any of the rest, but would like to point out that some of these examples have not been dealt with in their books or a few others I own. They are just a sampling of errors I've spotted, committed by people I had hoped would know better.

Many, possibly most, people have a problem with the distinction between *forte* and *forte*. I can't imagine why. *Forte* is Italian. In English, it is a musical instruction to get loud, and is pronounced "fortay". *Forte* is French. In English it means a strong point, as in "Math is my forte". It is pronounced "fort" — or should be. Virtually no one knows this. I am still puzzling over a line in a TV situation comedy from maybe a decade ago. One character says something is his forte, pronouncing it "fort". The other says "That's "fortay" — trust me — I used to be an English teacher". I like to think the line was written by someone who knew the distinction and was making a crack at teachers, but I'm probably wrong.

An indication of the problems that result when people learn English by watching TV can be seen in the proliferation of messed-up idioms written for print. One of my favourites is "all intensive purposes". Many people write "Here, here" for "Hear, hear", and vice versa. I have yet to read "Here, hear" or "Hear, here", but I am waiting. Yuppie MPs of recent decades have started shouting "Right on!" instead of "Hear, hear!", and that may be a good thing. If people would start saying "Watch it, Buster!" instead of "Here, here!" we might be able to put this whole problem behind us.

Some of the following may seem improbable, but I have seen, always more than once, such abominations as "nether-nether world [or land]", "Low and behold!", "in the throws of", "they are looking for an escape goat", "I don't like being second guest", "they have deep-seeded prejudices", "I tried a different tact", and many others that are, in a way, amusing as well as appalling. What they have in common, apart from the fact that they have been learned by ear rather than by reading, is that the people who write them are just parroting them, rather than thinking about what they are writing. I read recently that the civil service is a "yolk" on the back of the taxpayers. Some others: *weather* for *whether, jive* for *jibe* for *gibe, flack* for *flak, payed* for *paid, aloud* for *allowed, adds* for *ads, dispersed* for *disbursed, pore* for *pour, roll-playing, black-on-white* confused with *black-and-white, baited* for *bated, bantered* for *bandied* about, *flare* for *flair,* and *fare* for *fair.* I saw a bit of advice to drivers: "It's not advisable to try and break out of a skid." I've seen many educated people write "You've peeked [or peaked] my curiosity". Does that strike a familiar cord with you?

It isn't only a faulty ear that leads to confused idioms. I have seen someone write of "a frog in my throat" when he obviously meant lump. Folklore has it that if you tie a stick to a donkey's head and dangle a carrot from the end of the stick, the donkey will walk forward in vain pursuit of the carrot. This is known as the "carrot-on-a-stick" approach. People who don't know any better have corrupted this to the "carrot-and-stick" approach, which seems to mean something, but not anything very interesting.

You can blame the influence of TV for many things, but not for the like of *heresy* for *hearsay, lose* for *loose, adverse* for *averse,* and hundreds of others.

I am fully aware of the distinction between *alternatively* and *alternately,* yet I sometimes type the wrong one. Hell, I quite often type *it's* for *its,* although that error is one of my pet hates. These are the things that keep me humble and grateful for editors.

A U.S. tax reform activist being interviewed on TV made much of the "need to cut the duplicity of government services". I imagine the line was appreciated by much of his audience, but I suspect that he meant to say "duplication".

The CBC news told us about "one of the many indignations suffered by the hostages". The same day it mentioned that a politician had "diverted from his script". I think the CBC should know such words as *indignities* and *diverged,* as well as the difference between *singular* and *single,* the confusion of which is surprisingly frequent.

I have noticed in TV newscasts, but not in print, a tendency to confuse *instances* with *instants* with *incidents* with *incidence(s)*. This is too sorry a mess to try to comment on. The same people stumble over *instantly* and *instantaneously* and may use *estimation* for *estimate,* and are almost certain to say *at the bequest of* when they mean *at the behest of.* Some of them seem unaware that there is a difference between a shadowy character and a shady person. Others would not bother to look up the difference between *repelled* and *repulsed.* They would not be sure whether they are perpetrating these errors or perpetuating them. They probably are doing both. If accused, they would make an admittance of guilt.

Careless pronunciation combined with careless diction makes it difficult to confirm one's suspicion that a speaker is confusing *diffuse* with *defuse* (or *de-fuse,* if you prefer), but I have seen a lawyer quoted in print as saying, "I'm trying to diffuse a situation between a mom and dad who have kids to raise". Now, a dangerous situation could be diffused, meaning made more widespread, or it could be defused, meaning made harmless. I have tried dozens, if not hundreds, of times to discern which of these two words is actually being spoken by heads of state or pundits or anyone else. And when I see either in print, I'm still not sure if someone is being quoted correctly, or if the reporter even knows the difference. I'm sure I have heard Brian Mulroney confuse the two.

A well-meaning reader once gave me a severe headache by sending me a clipping from *The Toronto Star* in which a columnist, attacking Margaret Trudeau's book *Consequences,* stated that it is "a book that taxes one's credibility with every half-hearted turn of the page".

Certainly that is a deplorable misuse of *credibility*, which is the quality of deserving to be believed. It is the credibility of the book that is in question, not that of the reader. It should be enough merely to point that out and then go on to something else. But the person who sent the clipping felt compelled to suggest that the correct word would be *credulity*.

That might satisfy most, but it must be pointed out that *credulity* does not just mean (as it did long ago) readiness to believe; it denotes excessive readiness to believe, or gullibility, and has done so for two centuries. So it doesn't quite serve in this context. And the headache came on when I started trying to think of a word that would, by itself, correct the sentence. I have given up, but the headache remains. I don't know how *credulity* acquired its pejorative sense, but when it did we lost a useful term that has not, in 200 years, been replaced. (Not, at least, to my knowledge.)

Still picking away at the subject, I must note that *incredulity* continues to mean what it has always meant. It is a precise antonym of *credulity* in the obsolete sense of the latter word, but not in the modern sense.

Despite all this, I suspect that the misguided columnist was confusing *credibility* with *credulity*, a thesis that led me to consult *Room's Dictionary of Confusibles*, which, coincidentally, had just arrived in the mail that day. Sure enough, Room says *credible* and *credulous* are frequently confused, one for the other, but he also makes it clear that *credulous* means gullible.

Room, who is Adrian Room, a British lexicographer and geographer of note, has let me down once or twice since I acquired his dictionary. He was no help with *exult* and *exalt*, for instance. And obviously he has never felt the frustration of trying to get *disparate measures* into print without some green copy editor changing it to *desperate measures*; not written *causal relationship* only to have it come out in print as *casual relationship*. But he does list some 800 "confusibles", which he deals with deftly and concisely. With Room around, no one need ever again confuse *discomfort* with *discomfit* or *misuse* for *abuse*. He does nothing for us that a good general dictionary would not do, but his slim volume delivers its limited services at a considerable saving of the user's time and effort. And idle moments spent leafing through its pages might help any of us to avoid confusing or being confused in the future.

I've spent a lot of time over the years wondering how to avoid the pain in the neck brought on by the distinction between *immigrate* and *emigrate,* and between their corresponding nouns. We all know that one emigrates from somewhere and that to immigrate is to move into a new place. But since you can't leave one place without coming into another, is the distinction really necessary? Does one have to say "He emigrated from Canada and immigrated into Germany"? One can say correctly and more simply that he migrated from Canada to France. But what do you call him? Is he a French immigrant and a Canadian emigrant, or is it the other way 'round? In common speech, we speak of someone who came here from France as a French immigrant. That must be wrong, but that's what we say.

Furthermore, we can no longer get around it by calling the fellow a migrant. Newer dictionaries warn us that *migrant* as a noun carries the pejorative suggestion that the person so labelled is one who flits hither and yon; one who is something of a gypsy; a migratory worker.

If only everyone would just stay put...

A somewhat simpler distinction is the one between *come* and *go* and their various forms, but even that seems too much for many writers to grasp. Time and again you will find someone writing in Canada for Canadians that, say, an American who had been living

in Vancouver "came back" to Los Angeles. That one leaves me
baffled, but there is the possibility of reasonable confusion between
the two. You might tell your boss you're going home and then call
your wife and probably say you're coming home. You could be pardoned for not knowing whether you're coming or going.

Imagine you are doing a crossword puzzle and are faced with
SP_ _IOUS, and the definition is "counterfeit". If you are as easily
confused as I, you might turn to your copy of *Room*, wherein you
would find neither *spurious* nor *specious*. (The trouble with Room
is that he is obviously not as easily confused as many of us; only 800
pairs or groups of words in all the language confused him sufficiently to merit inclusion in his dictionary.)

　　Were I confronted with such a puzzle (fortunately, I have not
been), I'd probably choose *spurious*, but not before looking up
both words in a conventional dictionary, as I still have to do every
time I want to use either word. You might say that both words are
very similar, but I hope you'd leave out the *very*. *Spurious* is a reasonably straightforward word from the Latin for bastard or illegitimate, and it still carries the basic meaning of having an illegitimate
or irregular origin. *Specious*, on the other hand, is a more beguiling
word. Its original meaning of beautiful to behold or fair in appearance survived the move from Latin to Middle English, but later it
came to mean showy or flashy, and then beautiful in appearance
only. Eventually, the *OED* assigned it the meaning of "having a fair
or attractive appearance but in reality devoid of the qualities apparently possessed". And *spurious* is defined as "superficially resem-
bling or simulating but lacking the genuine characteristics or qualities of something".

　　It is quite common to see *specious* used to describe counterfeit
money or other objects, and it also is common for writers who use

it thus to be told that they are wrong; that they mean *spurious*. But, apart from the fact that *specious* implies a compliment to the skill of the counterfeiter, it seems to me quite correct to apply it to any successful forgery. While the two words are not generally interchangeable, they are similar, and I say they belong in anybody's dictionary of confusibles.

It isn't difficult to understand how such pairs as *flounder* and *founder*, *flout* and *flaunt*, and *career* and *careen* are confused, but I wonder about the likes of *cogent* and *germane*. I suppose it's because both are applied to arguments, but a cogent argument is a convincing one and a germane one is to the point, and the distinction is often missed.

Envision is a neologism recognized by *Webster* but not by the *OED*. It means to imagine something that does not exist, or to picture in the mind. *Envisage*, Fowler says, is a vogue word imported from France and pretentiously used as a substitute for several more precise terms. It is not necessary to choose between them. Neither has a unique meaning; both are imprecise.

Many people have difficulty with the verbs *career* and *careen*, and not without cause. The latter originally meant lay a ship on its side for repairs. By extension, it came to be an intransitive verb meaning list to one side, then, perhaps from side to side. It may be used to suggest a swaying or reeling progression. To *career* is to proceed at speed, usually through or over a course. A motorist indifferent to speed signs might career through a small town; if taken in drink, he might both career and careen through it. A skier might career through the slalom, although he could not do it without careening. One might careen through a career, but one cannot career through a careen. The words resemble each other somewhat to the eye and ear, and this is one of the trickier pairs of confusibles, and it would be a blessing if those ignorant of the distinction would avoid using either word. This advice is extended to the hordes of professional writers who misuse both these words. Many of them also think *careen* means carom. It doesn't.

Once I was threatened with a libel action by a lawyer who charged, in a letter of intent, that I had "imputed his client's motives". I could only guess what he might have meant by that. I had, in fact, imputed certain motives to his client and then impugned those motives. I surmised that a lawyer who didn't know the difference between *impute* and *impugn* might easily be fended off with a burst of bafflegab. I was right.

Here's a problem that doesn't bother speakers, but often confuses the journalists who report the speeches. A mediator in a labour dispute might say that he had made a *discreet* proposal to the union leader. Or did he say *discrete*? He might mean that he had quietly suggested something to the union man without letting management know. That would be *discreet*. Or perhaps he had made a proposal that was quite apart and distinct from whatever else was being negotiated, or one comprising several unrelated elements, in either of which cases the word would be *discrete*. A printed report using the inappropriate spelling could mislead the reader, no matter how he might pore (not pour) over it.

Some errors in the choice of words are quite obvious. You might have to stop and think for a moment, but you can usually tell what was meant. Others can create real confusion. When the CBC's noted interviewer the late Barbara Frum (who used to drive me up

the wall by consistently pronouncing *consortium* "consorteeum")
at least once said "insoluble problems" instead of "unsolvable
problems", she was committing a fairly common error, and there is
no problem in solving the little puzzle she posed. If you were talking about efforts to dissolve oil in water, possibly you could say you
have an insoluble problem as well as an unsolvable problem, but
that wasn't the case. If something is solvable, it can be solved. If it is
soluble, it can be dissolved. No big deal.

Enervate has a rough life. It means weaken, or deprive of force
or strength. Probably more often than not these days it is used, by
people who should know better, to mean precisely the opposite. It
has never been one of our most common words, and I suppose
people who misuse it think they have found an elegant variation of
energize, which is a common word (perhaps too common for
them) and is rarely misused or misunderstood. *Enervate* is close to
being a dead duck. I don't know if it's significant that politicians
seem particularly prone to this error. I've also spotted a few MPs
who don't seem to know the difference between *dearth* and *glut*, or
who don't know that *fulsome* is a pejorative word. One of them misused *fulsome* in the same speech in which he misused *enervate*. Politicians also have an inclination to use *expound on* for *expand on*,
and *expatiate* for *explain*.

I had difficulty in deciding in which chapter to place a discussion of
the *that/which* distinction. It involves a variety of problems. Since
one of these is that people often wrongly use *which* in place of *that*,
this seemed as good a place as any.

An acquaintance in the editing caper has drawn my attention to
the opening sentence of a subscription-renewal notice from a magazine for children: "Last year you sent a present to a child that,
unlike so many others, brought pleasure all year long."

At a glance, it might appear amusing, if you think that *that,* because of proximity, could refer to *child* rather than *present.* In reality, no gentleperson would use *that* to refer to another person, save with intent to disparage, but there is nothing here to suggest that the writer is incapable of inelegance.

This is one way of getting into the *that/which* problem. I was well into middle age before I really tackled it, and I'm still not sure I've wrestled it to the ground. I know some good writers and editors who have gone all their lives without getting a good handle on it and some others who are not even aware of the distinction.

Yet the rule, if you can believe most authorities, is simple. The relative pronoun *that* is defining or restrictive; *which* is non-defining or non-restrictive, and that's that.

It would be well to define *defining,* I guess. A defining (restrictive) clause specifically identifies the antecedent of *that,* as in "The book that I want to read next is on the bedside table". A non-defining (non-restrictive) clause simply adds information about the antecedent of *which,* as in "The history book, which I want to read next, is on the bedside table".

It is also important to remember that a non-restrictive clause (beginning with *which*) should be separated with commas, while the restrictive clause (beginning with *that*) should *not.* Violations of this rule pose particular difficulties for the discerning reader. If a clause beginning with *which* is inserted without the commas, the reader has to figure out whether you are wrong about the *which* or wrong about the commas.

It's good to know that a rule that can be so simply stated will solve this problem, which has been bothering me for years. It's also good to know that this rule, which can be so simply stated, will solve this problem that has been bothering me for years.

What I would really like to know is why, if it's so damn' simple, the article devoted to the question is, at five pages, one of the longest (and most confusing) in Fowler's book.

He does say, succinctly, that "if writers would agree to regard *that* as the defining relative pronoun, and *which* as the non-defining, there would be much gain both in lucidity and in ease". But he admits that this is not the practice "either of most or of the best of writers". He also admits that the rule is not always easy for others to follow. (One gets the impression that *nothing* is too difficult for Fowler.)

My own difficulty with *that* and *which* is aggravated by the fact that I am stuck with one of those spurious rules that plague us all. Some long-forgotten mentor evidently impressed upon my mind the fallacy that says that *that* is a colloquial relative that should be replaced by *which* in written English. That is simply wrong.

The fallacy, Fowler says, stems from the fact that *which* is more often demanded by the complex constructions of written sentences than by the simple ones of everyday speech, and, observing the frequent written use of *which*, many people conclude, wrongly, that it is the preferred form of *that*. "This false inference", he says, "tends to verify itself by persuading the writers who follow rules of thumb actually to change the original *that* of their thoughts into a *which* for presentation in print."

That last is an ungenerous remark. A person who has had a wrong precept drilled into him at an early age, and who has tried without total success to uproot it, should not be accused of "following" rules of thumb, dammit. Even in writing the above paragraphs I caught myself several times starting a defining clause with *which*. It's a lapse which frequently defies my best efforts at vigilance.

Furthermore, Mr. Fowler (would that you were still with us), given the complexity of the various problems that *that* poses, upon which you expatiate so volubly, and considering how much more difficult it all becomes if that other tricky relative, *who*, is brought into the discussion, is it not possible that your simple rule, quoted above, could be said to be one of thumb? Put which in your pipe and smoke it!

I can only say (correctly) that the habit of misusing *which*, which is a bad one, is a habit that I will try to break.

I broached the *that/which* problem here, pretending, with my innate cowardice, that it could be treated by itself, but actually, it's the *that/which/who* problem. The *who* makes it stickier, and I can't ignore it altogether.

I'm not the first person to turn chicken on the subject. In *The Careful Writer,* Theodore Bernstein frets at length over *that/which*, but dismisses *that/which/who* by quoting a grade-school saw: "*Which* normally refers to things, *who* to persons, and *that* to either persons or things", to which he adds "The point is elementary and needs no elaboration".

That is amusing, because Bernstein draws heavily on Fowler for his *that/which* essay but when it comes to *who*, he suddenly goes blind. Fowler, having dealt with *that/which* with little evidence of strain, goes on to agonize about *who*:

> It would be satisfactory if the same clear division of func-
> tions that can be confidently recommended for *that* and
> *which*, viz. between defining and non-defining clauses,
> could be established also for *that* and *who*; this would give
> us *that* for all defining clauses whether qualifying persons or
> things, and *who* for persons but *which* for things in all non-
> defining.

There are no real rules here. In general, *who* serves well in reference to one human or more, but *that* is by no means ruled out. The two can be interchanged to achieve effective nuances, but Bernstein's rule of thumb is not a bad one.

Things get ugly when collectives are involved. That problem has more to do with collectives than with *that/which/who*, but it certainly is a problem. I know of no easier way to find an example of it than to read or listen to a few business news reports, which are replete with atrocities of this type: "General Motors is expected to announce a cutback in production of their heavy trucks. Its board of directors says their decision was inevitable because the UAW is refusing to lower their wage demands." And so on.

Let's see you stick a *who* or *which* or *that* clause into *that* story.

So the whole *which/that/who* area is a swamp, but you can usually get through it safely with the aid of a little logic.

The experts in stylistics tell us that one of the greatest problems facing the communicator is that of defining the audience. The writer of the letter quoted in the introduction to this topic, soliciting a renewal of a magazine subscription, was not a student of stylistics. Indeed, I doubt that the writer was even aware of being technically illogical.

What I would have demanded, had I been the employer of that writer, would have been his or her awareness that the letter would be read by some doting donor who bought the original subscription in the hope that it would encourage the small recipient to be a reader, and that, therefore, the donor might be put off by the *perception* of careless writing on behalf of the publisher.

And, indeed, that is what happened. The subscription was allowed to lapse.

I am tired of being "corrected" by Torontonians when I refer to my laneway. I come from a Nova Scotia family and did much of my growing up in Ottawa, and in such places people know the difference between a lane (or laneway) and a driveway, as do all respectable dictionaries. What I have is a *laneway*, which runs between two houses and provides access to the rear of the property. Torontonians call this a *driveway*. They are wrong. A driveway is a sort of road that provides access between a thoroughfare and the entrance to a building. Toronto people are wrong about a lot of things, in case you hadn't noticed.

The conventional wisdom is that we should say *between* two and *among* three or more. I would be happy to oblige, but it just isn't that simple. This is one of those rules of thumb, so loved by minor pedagogues, that Fowler calls "superstitions" or "fetishes". I was taught it in school, and I dare say you were, too. But it doesn't serve. The *OED* goes on and on about it, making it one of those subjects I wish I hadn't looked up. If you and a group of your friends wish to discuss the matter between yourselves, that's okay with the *OED*. At election time, you may have a choice between three candidates, not among them. *Among* suggests belonging. If you fall among thieves, you become one of them. If three thieves surround you and knock you down, you fall between them. It is not correct to speak of "a rose among thorns" and it is not poetic to speak of "a rose between thorns". That's your problem. No doubt the best thing to do is keep in mind that the rule of thumb is generally but not invariably applicable.

I have noticed lately that people are doing less expecting and more anticipating. That is alarming. There is no justification at all for the use of *anticipate* as a synonym for *expect*. To anticipate something is to foresee it, and, usually, to forestall it, or at least attempt to forestall it. It is that sense that makes the word valuable. *Expect* is a good word. Most people know what it means. That, I suppose, is why some writers shun it. A woman who expects to have a baby probably will, but a woman who anticipates having a baby can expect to arouse the wrath of the right-to-life crowd, an eventuality she could anticipate by not anticipating childbirth.

There are hundreds of confusibles. Perhaps their misuse by professional communicators can sometimes be blamed on heterophemy; more often it is the result of a lack of professionalism.

(Okay, I was going to just let that one ride, but, because it is a useful word, I'll say that *heterophemy* is the unconscious saying or writing of words other than those intended. The significant word there is *unconscious.* I guess we all do it once in a while. That's just one more reason we all need editors.)

CHAPTER 13

Idiosyncrasies

All languages pose many odd little problems, not to mention some odd big ones. Some think English is a world leader in this respect. Could be. Let's take a look at a tiny number of them.

One of the most intriguing, albeit certainly not the most useful, books I have read on English usage is *Paradigms Lost,* by the critic John Simon, in which he repeatedly snarls that people who say *intriguing* when they mean *fascinating* are fools. I flushed guiltily, but went off to check four reputable sources, two of which agreed with Simon and two of which placidly accepted fascinate as one meaning of *intrigue.* However, I am inclined to agree with Simon: *intrigue* should not have its denotations of clandestine romancing or secret plotting watered down by such careless use.

Anyway, although I would not give the acerbic Simon the last word on any topic, I would recommend the book. Subtitled *Reflections on Literacy and Its Decline,* it is suffused with the sort of deep concern for the welfare of the language that you find in such other best-sellers on the subject as those of William Safire and Edwin

Newman. It isn't as much fun, but there is some satisfaction in discovering that Simon, for all his dogmatic blustering, is still one of those of us who live in glass houses. He writes:

> The term "functional illiterate" designates someone who, although he can technically read and write, cannot do it well enough to be a fully functioning member of our society. In other words, you [sic] cannot read road signs or the instructions on a medicine jar and draw the correct inferences. Yet even these frequently adduced examples of functional illiteracy ought to point to an inescapable conclusion: what good is reading and writing to people who cannot think?

I put it to you, Simon, that a question is not a conclusion, but, if it is, my conclusion is: how did *he* become *you* between sentences?

Someone once wrote me to report that her 1925 Ontario high-school grammar says that "each other is always used with reference to two, and one another is used with reference to more than two", and she asked if this rule had been discarded. I don't believe it ever was a rule, except in the mind of the author of that book, who should have written *sometimes* instead of *always.* Says Fowler: "This differentiation is neither of present utility nor based on historical usage." And so another schoolteachers' superstition bites the dust. I wonder if Matthew Arnold, had he been educated in Ontario, would have written (in "Dover Beach"), "Ah, love, let us be true / To each other!" and thereby spoiled his metre.

As a young reporter, I worked for some time at a desk adjacent to that of an experienced writer who held an honours degree in English and for whom I had great respect and liking, despite her lifelong inability to grasp the distinction between the possessive *your* and the contraction *you're*. I didn't realize then that I would spend the rest of my life bumping into what I still consider an inexplicable blind spot.

Contractions, of course, have no place in written English, or so I've been told by some purists. They do seem to be at the root of many problems that might dismay the inventor of the apostrophe, who doubtless had only the best of intentions. They can be blamed for the loss of the *shall/will* distinction.

There are more problems with contractions. There is the infamous *alright*. What do you say to someone who asks why, if it is all right to write *already*, it is not all right to write *alright*? You will get nowhere trying to explain that *all ready* does not have the same meaning as *already* and that there is not, and there need not be, such a word as *alright*. A possible response to such a lecture might be a Runyonesque "Awright, awready". (Despite the way his characters spoke, Damon Runyon was an astute grammarian who once wrote a memorable diatribe about Cole Porter's lyrics, particularly the line from "Night and Day": "I've got you under the hide of me.") It should also be noted that *all together* and *altogether* are not interchangeable, either.

An editor of my acquaintance reports an increase in the use of *anyone* for *any one*, as in *at anyone moment*; of *awhile* for *a while*, as in *awhile ago*; of *anymore*; and, God help us, of *alot* for *a lot*, which I find hard to believe, even today.

When I was a lad, *anymore* was not a word. *Any more* could mean something like *nowadays*, which is what *anymore* means today, but it could, and still can, mean something else, as in "I will not put up with any more of this nonsense". I suppose this is progress, but the thing that bothers me about it is that while *any more*, as two words, is in the good old *Webster,* the newer dictionaries make it apparent that the phrase doesn't exist anymore. The upshot is that we are already seeing it written in such contexts as "I don't want anymore broccoli".

Many of these errors and confusions could be avoided by applying common sense. A homicide detective or a madam would understand the difference between *anybody* and *any body* or *somebody* and *some body*; why can't a reporter make the same distinction, and why can't we get across to the writers who nowadays tend to leave the apostrophe out of *can't* that *cant* is a word in its own right?

There is a little-observed distinction between *half a dozen* and *a half-dozen*. The former suggests that there is a dozen of something, and this is half of it. A half-dozen is six. If you have an aversion to saying *six* (possibly for fear that some Tixan will think you're talking about sex) you can say *a half-dozen*, and I won't get on your back. It's six of one and a half-dozen (but not half a dozen) of the other, for all I care. In the same ballpark, it should be noted that cutting something in half means cutting it into two equal segments; otherwise you're cutting it in two, not in half.

One day when I was listening, not at all carefully, to a U.S. network TV newscast there was an item, as usual, about violence following a quasi-funeral in South Africa. My ear was suddenly jarred by a line referring to a man "who, many say, has become a martyr".

I thought that was a peculiar, and possibly even stupid, thing to say, and I was soon at the keyboard writing something to the effect that a martyr is a martyr, and that it was irrelevant in this context whether many or few or none or all *say* that he is. I was also bothered by the *become*. It seemed to carry the implication that becoming a martyr is a gradual process; that it is a title bestowed by some sort of popular consensus.

In fact, except in the narrow, ecclesiastical sense, becoming a martyr is an action taken voluntarily by the martyr-to-be. The "modern" meaning of the noun has been established for centuries. The *OED* cites a 1650 reference to "that heathen martyr Socrates", which is amusing in itself, because *martyr* in the time of Socrates was a Greek word meaning witness. (That, in turn, is a clue to how it came through religious channels to its present meaning in English.)

For a valid modern definition, I like the following from *Webster*: "One who sacrifices his life, station, or what is of great value, for the sake of principle, or to sustain a cause." That is clear enough for me.

No doubt you have discerned how I was sitting here smearing egg all over my face. One jaw of the trap I had fallen into was my willingness, if not eagerness, to believe that when anything in a news report strikes me as peculiar it is probably because of careless writing; the other was my allowing myself to get so caught up in that detail that I had not really paid attention to the context. I had simply, and stupidly, said to myself: "Here is a man who gave his life to uphold the cause of anti-apartheid; he is, by definition, a martyr." I had not even bothered to note his identity.

I had written quite a lot before I stopped to wonder whether it might be barely possible that the reporter had written that restrictive clause for some good reason that I had missed. I dug into memory, and then into the press, and discovered that the man referred to was Benjamin Moloise, who, although known as a firm supporter of the violent overthrow of apartheid, had in fact been, rightly or wrongly, hanged for murder. I read that he had confessed, then recanted, then admitted that he had become involved in planning the crime out of fear for his own life.

So, in truth, the reporter was doing his job well by writing "who, many say, has become a martyr", because there certainly is room for argument whether he is a martyr or not.

I felt like a bloody fool, and did the electronic equivalent of tearing up what I'd written. But I found no comfort in the fact that I alone knew of the blunder. I can endure any kind of criticism except self-criticism, and I just couldn't leave this alone. This isn't the first time I have caught myself this way, and I keep hoping to learn. The lesson for me is: before you call the kettle black, suck in your pot. The lesson for you may well be: always keep a comfortable distance between yourself and anyone showing symptoms of autocatharsis.

Following the imposition of some despotic regulation by the Canadian Radio-television and Telecommunications Commission, my local cable-TV company once posted this on-screen message: "Pay-TV is available in stereo for C-Channel music programs only at this time."

Here is the pesky *only* at its worst. Anyone who had been following the news about pay-TV would have understood the intended meaning of the message almost immediately. Anyone else would not have cared. And anyone who had pointed out that the *only* in that sentence belonged between "for" and "C-Channel" would have been termed a pedantic bore by most (and already has been by some).

But this must be pursued. The *only* could have been dropped into several comfortable spots in that sentence (and a couple of uncomfortable ones) without causing great confusion to the intended recipients of the message. But in some other places, it might have befuddled many. The writer who thought he had placed it where it belonged would, I doubt not, have thought it equally efficient to place it between "stereo" and "for". It would have been no more confusing there.

It is a bad sentence. But, as it stands, there is only one proper location in it for *only*.

The wrong placement of this word is one of the most common errors in English syntax. I commit it frequently, and I'd bet that you do, too. It's so common, indeed, that we tend to condone its commission by the "you-know-what-I-mean" types, and feel it incumbent on us to figure out (often without much difficulty) just what was meant, and not to complain about it.

Even Fowler is uncommonly permissive about its placement. In a rather remarkable diatribe he rants about pedants whose "design is to force us all, whenever we use the adverb *only*, to spend time in considering which is the precise part of the sentence strictly qualified by it, and then put it there — this irrespective of whether there is any danger of the meaning's being false or ambiguous..." He does go on. It would seem he had become enraged by some piece of pedantry even more arrogant than the one he cites at the beginning of the article. It's worth looking up, because you'll seldom find him so splenetic.

Eventually he calms down enough to offer this advice:

> There is an orthodox position for the adverb, easily determined in case of need; to choose another position that may spoil or obscure the meaning is bad; but a change of position that has no such effect except technically is not only justified by historical and colloquial usage but often demanded by rhetorical needs.

After all the ranting, he is saying what is eminently reasonable: put *only* where it seems to you to look or sound good, but be sure you're making your meaning clear. Orthodoxy should not destroy style, but style should not destroy clarity.

Still, we all should stick a red flag on *only*, and never use it without thinking, not about orthodoxy, but about the possibility of being misunderstood. I've never wondered what the songwriter meant by "I only have eyes for you", and I wouldn't for the world have had him desert style for orthodoxy and write "I have eyes for only you", or even "for you only".

Theodore Bernstein, an authority who has been known to nod but whose advice is generally plain and sensible, is of some help in this matter. He allows that the "normally" proper position for *only* is adjacent to (and usually preceding) whatever it qualifies, but then goes on to list a bewildering number of exceptions. He does recommend "developing an *only* awareness", and cites a useful exercise: "Eight different meanings result from placing *only* in the eight possible positions in this sentence: 'I hit him in the eye yesterday.'" Try it for yourself, then tell me again that it's pedantic to demand that writers take time to think about possible ambiguity every time they use that word.

Bernstein should have stopped there. Obviously, once a writer has developed his "*only* awareness", he will avoid using the word ambiguously. It's equally obvious that too many writers either have not developed that awareness or are not qualified for their jobs (although this is so pervasive a trap that anyone must be excused for an *occasional* lapse — and how's that for a cop-out?).

I transmitted a couple of examples of *only* misuse for the consideration of users of an international computer conference of writers. The most interesting revisions that came back were from writers who had deftly rewritten the sentences and eliminated the *only*s with no loss of clarity and vigour. Anyone finding that proper placement of the word is awkward and that improper placement causes ambiguity would be well advised to consider not using it at all.

Bernstein doesn't help matters when he goes on to say that *only* may be used as a conjunction in place of *but*, "although the use is more appropriate to speech than to writing", but that it should not be used in place of *except*. I venture to suggest that its use in place of *but* is more appropriate to gutter speech than to polite converse.

A reader of *Books in Canada* once wrote to accuse me of using no fewer than four infelicities in one column. Had he called them mistakes, I would have bridled, but I like the word *infelicity*. I had used *gotten*, which is an alternative past participle (along with *got*) of *get*. It is frowned on in England, but the Americans are tolerant of it. I am more than tolerant of it. I like it, in certain constructions, have gotten used to using it, and will go on using it long after that letter is forgot. It provides, I think, a useful distinction. If I tell you that I have got a new VCR, I might as well leave out the *got* and say I have a new VCR, but if I use *gotten*, I am saying I have performed the act of getting, or acquiring, it.

Then he hit me for saying something like "while *gotten* is frowned on in England, it is tolerated in America". He contended that I should have used *although*, not *while*. I'll accept that as an infelicity, but not as a mistake. Next, it was *end up*. I won't buy that even as an infelicity. You can find my defence in a discussion of "verb tails" later in this chapter. The fourth "infelicity" was no such thing. I had referred to having been "dumped on" for misusing a word. He was correct in saying that *dump* requires a direct object — in its formal sense. In slang, *dump* is an intransitive verb, meaning defecate, and, I suggest, is a damn sight more felicitous than the more common dysphemism. Vulgar? Perhaps. Infelicitous? Ah, c'mon, gimme a break.

One evening while I was half watching TV, my wandering attention was abruptly brought back to an interview when I heard the then U.S. vice-president George Bush say: "The United States can't do nothing." I was already jotting the line down when I realized he had said exactly what he meant, which was that, in the situation being discussed, it was impossible for the United States to avoid taking some sort of action. It was not a felicitous phrase, but it did command attention.

I would like now to address myself to the problem of those who speak of "addressing a problem", a phrase popular with MPs. To address something is to direct it, and you cannot address a problem. (Oh, I suppose you could put it in an envelope and address it to someone you don't like, or you could make a speech to it in the hope that it would go away.) You can address your attention to it, or address your efforts toward solving it.

There was a scene in Jackie Gleason's old television series, *The Honeymooners*, in which Ralph Kramden, while instructing Ed Norton in golf, ordered him to address the ball, whereupon Norton said, "Hello, ball", thereby proving himself smarter than not only Kramden but many politicians, too.

I once got myself into trouble by writing that English, for all its orthographic peculiarities, syntactic awkwardness, ambiguities, and general cussedness, frequently responds much more graciously to the application of common sense than to the application of classroom fetishes. A couple of my pet hates (discussed elsewhere) are *try and do* and *different than*, both of which offend me chiefly because they don't make sense. Still, I insist that a great many of the apparent illogicalities in our language do make sense in some way, if you look for it.

In the bars in which writers gathered in the 1980s there was much loud discussion over what to call one of the things Pierre Trudeau was doing to us. Was it metrification or metrication? I know of no authority to which we can turn on this one. I favour *metrication* simply because I can't find it in any dictionary. I can find *metrification*, and it means putting something into metrical form, not into metric form. Metrification is almost the same as versification. It has to do with the metre of language, not the metre of 39.37 inches. And since metrification already does mean something, it seems far more sensible (and justifiable by precedent) to coin *metricate* and *metrication* than to mess up the clear meaning of *metrify* and its forms. (I am also vaguely hostile to changing the spelling to *meter*, as in the U.S., but I can't call up any powerful arguments, and it's a lost cause, anyway.)

Someone asked me once why I was seeking some bit of arcane information. I started to reply that it was because I am a curious person. This was in writing, so I was able to change *curious* to *inquisitive* when I realized that, in this context, my use of *curious* could mean I am inquisitive (which was what I wanted it to mean), or it could mean I am queer (which was not what I wanted it to mean).

Curious is one of those damnably ambiguous words with which our language is riddled, and it might as well be chucked out. The *OED* is quite blunt about it, calling it "a word which [*sic*] has been used from time to time with many shades of meaning...".

It started out to mean something like painstaking. Chaucer used it that way, and it retained that meaning for four centuries after him. But even in his own time it was already ambiguous; to some writers it meant nosy. And, some 300 years ago, it began to be used to mean strange.

Of the eighteen meanings defined by the *OED*, only two have any currency today, but those two are enough to make it a dangerous word. Although they can be formally distinguished as subjective and objective, they still may cause confusion. The same is true of *curiosity*. You might tell me that your neighbour has a certain curiosity. I would not know whether you meant that he is forever peeping through his or your curtains or that he has a five-legged dog.

However, the word may settle down, and we can take comfort from the fact that, thanks to the communications explosion, it no longer is necessary to wait through the centuries for a changed meaning to become established. It is possible that tomorrow night some semiliterate media star will decide that *curious* means polite, and by Christmas that will be its meaning.

The following paragraphs are from a column I wrote some years ago for *Books in Canada*. I have two reasons for quoting them here. One is that I want to raise the issue of the plural *none*, about which my conviction remains unaltered. The other is to illustrate the danger of tongue-in-cheek writing without trumpeting the fact that you are trying to elongate the nether members of your readers. The style offended some people, including the reader who sent me the clipping, and bewildered others. The approach probably blurred the message, which is one I feel fairly strongly about. Live and learn.

Someone sent me a clipping from her local newspaper in which the common misuse of *none* as a plural pronoun is energetically defended. It is of no interest to me, because my mind is made up. However, any among you in search of justification for slovenly habits of speech may take encouragement from it.

It cites Fowler, the *OED*, and five of those wretched dictionaries published in the United States of America. None of the citations impresses me. Fowler is quoted as saying: "It is a mistake to suppose that the pronoun is singular only and must at all costs be followed by singular verbs." In fact, Fowler goes on to say that "the *OED* explicitly states that plural construction is commoner". That cunningly omitted line makes a great difference.

Regular readers of this column will have observed that Fowler is frequently quoted here, but only when he agrees with me, and the fact is that I am getting awfully tired of him and his everlasting laxity. His revisers are worse.

The OED, as everyone (perhaps excepting a few citizens of the United States of America) knows — or perhaps it should be "as everyone *know*" — is for the most part a chronicle of the abuses the English language has suffered at the hands of the likes of Shakespeare and Milton, who had the ill fortune to be writing before the rules of usage had been codified properly.

No attention at all need be paid the rebellious colonial thinking of the hysterically revisionist lexicographers of the USA, who take childish delight in licensing the most bizarre perversions of the mother tongue.

The author of the article flaunts *The American Heritage Dictionary* as having the best explanation: "A plural verb should be used when *none* applies to more than one." Now there is as stupid a statement as you're likely to find anywhere, let alone in a dictionary. *None,* applied to more than one? Anyway, the point is simply that *none* means no one, and the fact that its misuse can be traced back more than 1,000 years, that its misuse is widespread, and that its misuse is condoned by many authorities, have nothing to do with the basic fact that IT IS A SINGULAR PRONOUN. Common commission does not mean an error ceases to be an error; it means that it is a common error. Tell me, if you will, that sometimes a plural *none* makes for more comfortable idiomatic expression and I'll go along with you. But neither

you nor Fowler *is* going to tell me that it's "a mistake to suppose that the pronoun is singular only". Wanna talk about
neither now? No, I suppose none of you *care.*

(The reference to *neither* has to do with another of my pet gripes,
the use of *nor* without a previous *neither,* as in "I will not seek the
nomination, nor will I run if nominated". That *nor* should be a
neither.)

There is a bit of doggerel that goes:

> I wish I may
> I wish I might
> have the wish
> I wish tonight.

I don't know where that came from or why, save for the sake of
metre and rhyme, the author chose to use both *may* and *might,* but
it's as good a way as any to get into a discussion of these two trou-
blesome words. Both evolved from the same root. Often one can be
swapped for the other without harm, but beware! This is one of the
trickiest distinctions in the language.

It is a subject that terrifies me and I'd rather eat broccoli than
attempt to deal with this. Many people have difficulty enough with
may and *can,* despite the fact that grade-school teachers drum the
simple distinction into generation after generation of ears: *can* has
to do with the ability or power to do something; *may* involves per-
mission to do it. (Historically, *may* once meant what *can* now
means under this rule, but for God's sake don't tell *anybody* that!)

There is no easy distinction between *may* and *might.* There is a
simple *grammatical* distinction — *might* is the past tense of *may* —
but that's really not all you need to know. It tells you that the correct

construction would be "Yesterday I thought I might kill myself; today I think I may not". But if you ask me "Are you going to the hockey game tonight?", I may say "I might go" or I might say "I may go" or I might (or may) tell you to mind your own business. Were you to repeat the question, I *might* (but definitely not *may*) give you a civil answer. Think about it.

Sometimes the two words can be interchanged with no loss of clarity; sometimes not. The late Eugene Forsey, that grand and tireless champion of proper usage, wrote an irate letter to *The Globe and Mail* about a report on an airline disaster. The reporter had written that a certain safety measure "may have saved hundreds of lives". That implied that hundreds of lives were saved by the measure, when, in fact, no lives were saved. Some *might* have been, had the measure been implemented, but it was not.

In other constructions, it's good to bear in mind that *may* suggests a greater degree of possibility than does *might*. It's not much help to go to the dictionary with this problem. A sense of idiom is what's needed, and the writer who does not have that might (or even may) be well advised to seek other employment.

Here is another example of a consequential misuse. In a story on the homosexual cannibal who captured headlines for weeks in the United States, CNN reported that there had been more calls to police than had been previously revealed, and that these calls "may have prevented as many as four more murders". That was just plain wrong. It suggests that four more murders were prevented, possibly as a result of the calls. What was actually meant was that, had police acted on the calls, the murders *might* have been prevented, and *might* was the word that should have been used.

You might want to give some thought to the fact that *maybe* is a well-established word. I've never heard or read *mightbe* as one word.

I used to hear from time to time from Ted Culp, the president of The Simplified Spelling Society Ov Canada (SSSC). I could not espouse the cause, but recognize that he has a right to pursue it.

It has been estimated that about 45,000 years have elapsed since humans began using graphic representations as a supplement to speech, and I am made nervous by those who suggest we adopt their specific formulae (and there are many such schemes) to alter, drastically and instantaneously, the product of forty-five millennia of evolution.

Spelling reformers have illustrious literary antecedents (George Bernard Shaw springs to mind), and they are honourably motivated. A person who wants to do something about an orthography that could permit (to use Shaw's classic example) *fish* to be spelled "ghoti" can't be dismissed as a crank. (If you are not familiar with that one, think about rouGH wOmen in acTIon.)

Some of the reforms sought by the SSSC have been implemented to a considerable extent already. Canadian newspapers have been using *-or* in preference to *-our* (as in *honor* and *labor*) for decades, but most other publishers have not followed suit.

But our orthographic peculiarities are of no small value in reminding us of the etymology and meaning of our words, and they sometimes keep us out of trouble with homophones. If people who now are considered (by some) to be relatively harmless when they write "nite" instead of *night* are allowed to go unchecked, how will we later distinguish between such real words as *might* and *mite*, or *right* and *rite* or *sight* and *site* and *cite*?

Once, when we were on the brink of a municipal election, my eye was caught (and offended) by a heading in a weekly newspaper that serves the municipal ward in which I live and vote. The heading read: "Everything that informed voters ought to know."

It was, indeed, a foolish caption. The feature that followed was

nothing more than an attempt to clarify a change in election procedure that had puzzled many of our burghers, and to catalogue
some other basic facts. It was useful information, but it wasn't
everything. I assume the word was used facetiously, but the frivolity
was out of place. However, what bothered me was the misuse of
informed. Surely *informed* voters already know what they ought to
know, and the information being offered is something *uninformed*
voters ought to know.

Does it *really* matter? Here was this friendly, free, little neighbourhood newspaper trying quite efficiently to help me through
the election maze, and all I could do was carp about a little slip that
virtually no one else would even notice, much less be misled by.
Nevertheless, to answer my own question, yes, it really matters.

I suspect that someone explained to me, when I was very young, the
meaning of "A friend in need is a friend indeed", because I would
have had no other way of knowing which of its two potential meanings was intended.

I use *end up* frequently, sometimes just to irritate people who have
chided me for it, but often for a better reason. *Up* is an idiomatic
but unnecessary tail for *end* in many cases, but, to cite an example
from Bernstein, try taking the *up* away from the statement "If a boy
cheats in school he will end up a criminal".

Bernstein goes on at some length about verb tails, but his basic
advice is simply to think about it. In some cases — *simmer down,
head off, single out* — the tail is obviously necessary. To *check on*
something is the same as to check it — in one sense of *check.* But the
word also means to stop, and if the context possibly permits misunderstanding, the tail should be kept. There is no need for the tails in
head up or *win out,* but *hurry up* and *slow down* are so well

established in our idiom that it seems a bit prissy to dock their tails. *Free up* perhaps is all right if you are speaking of throwing out some mouldy treasures from your attic to free up some storage space, but you wouldn't free up a prisoner.

A double one, which is doubly offensive, is *meet up with*. I have no problem with *steal away* by itself, as in "He stole away into the night", but when I notice writers talking about someone stealing something away from someone I get prickly. The millionaire CBS newscaster Dan Rather spoke of someone being "hired on". At such times, I think it's time Mr. Rather was hired off.

I got to know a chap whose speech habits mystified me somewhat for some time. His conversation was jammed with such useless lines as "so to speak", "as they say", and "if I may put it that way". The mystery dissolved when I discovered he had been brought to Canada as a young boy from an eastern European country, and it suddenly became obvious that he had learned English by listening to disc jockeys on private radio. He confirmed this once by looking at his wristwatch and announcing: "Well, the old clock on the wall says it's almost that time known as four o'clock, and I have to be getting outta here." Or something like that.

CHAPTER 14

Erosion Can Wear You Down

Conservationists might be well advised to divert some of their attention from cute little animals to the no less serious problem of the ongoing destruction of our means of understanding each other, but the fact is that they are contributing as much as anyone to the erosion of words. One day in the early 1960s, a noted ecologist I was interviewing pointed out to me that I had just misused *ecology*. The word refers to a branch of biology dealing with the relationship and interaction between organisms and their environment. It has now become quite common to speak of something — acid rain, say — as "posing a threat to the ecology".

It didn't bother me at all when ecologists and others started talking about the dreaded *greenhouse effect*. I thought it was an apt metaphor, but failed to see where it might lead. It has led to such phrases as *greenhouse gases*. That is an abomination. It is used to refer to gases that contribute to the greenhouse effect, but the only thing it could rationally mean is gases found in a greenhouse. It is frequently used by people who, I'd bet, don't even know what a greenhouse is.

One of the worst things that happen to words is the mindless adaptation of a perfectly good word to serve some unnecessary purpose other than the one God meant it to serve. When the misuse catches on, the word becomes useless. A good example is *presently,* whose meaning has varied over the centuries. Sometimes it meant now, sometimes it meant soon. Right now it means nothing. Of more immediate concern is *momentarily,* which for a long time meant for a moment, but which has lately been perverted to mean a moment from now. There is no need for this. *Presently* has at times served the purpose for which *momentarily* has been perverted. *Currently* still means what *presently* sometimes meant. If people wouldn't mess around so much, we would still be able to use *currently* to mean now, *presently* to mean soon, and *momentarily* to mean for a very brief period of time. Two of the three words have been made useless.

Possibly of less consequence is the fate of *decimate,* but it's a good illustration of how these things happen. Back around Shakespeare's time, it used to mean to reduce by one-tenth. I'll allow that perhaps many of us can live a full life without a word that means precisely that. But the process (which began in the last century) of its acquisition of the meaning destroy a great proportion of, say, an army, or a population, did not occur because someone had the bright idea that it wasn't being used much anyway so it might as well be used for something else. It occurred because the word was ignorantly misused by enough people that it took on a new meaning. All right, that's the way languages evolve. But a central point of all the verbiage in these pages is that, because of the so-called communications explosion, it's all happening too quickly now. Some oaf with a camera stuck in his face misuses a word, and millions of people who think he knows what he's talking about pick it up. Not long ago, Johnny Carson used *peccadilloes* to refer to someone's idiosyncrasies, and I just thought, hell, there goes another word. We'll see.

The lion's share has come to be used and understood to mean most. The phrase derives from one of Aesop's fables, and was formerly used as a colourful and ironic way of saying all. There is absolutely no point in using it in the sense it has acquired.

When the University of Toronto's new supercomputer was put into place, a CBC-TV reporter informed us that "scientists will spend a week hooking up reams of wire and cables". *Ream* is a unit of measurement of rather uncertain value, since it has denoted different numbers in different applications. Usually, it meant twenty quires, or 480 sheets, of paper. It was in one of those tables we were required to memorize when I was in school, but it is little used today. To a printer, say, a ream would not be a great deal of paper, but to someone writing on it with a quill pen (and to someone reading the result), it would be a lot. Not unreasonably, the plural form came, in colloquial use, to mean a great quantity of written material. It is absurd to use it in reference to what probably is miles of wire. (Some editors no doubt would change *miles* to *kilometres* here, but to hell with them.) I expect that soon I will read about someone drinking reams of beer.

A U.S. writer called the fifty-five-mile-per-hour speed limit "the most flaunted law in the land". I was about to shrug it off as another example of the common *flaunt/flout* confusion, but then reflected that if to *flaunt* something is to display it ostentatiously, well, there are those reams of speed-limit signs everywhere you look, and maybe it *is* the most flaunted law. Somehow, though, I think that the writer was innocent of any such sly wit.

Here are three words that are being destroyed. Some dictionaries will (or, if not read carefully, will seem to) condone their misuse.

Alibi does not mean excuse. Without going into a full legal definition, it is the fact or condition of being in a different place at a certain time. It is ridiculous to say a child does not have an alibi for
being late for school; obviously if he was not there he was somewhere else and does have an alibi. But it's not an excuse.

Value and *cost* are not synonymous. The value of something is
its worth; its cost is what you pay for it. Money is not necessarily
involved. A valuable experience may or may not be costly, and vice
versa.

Valuable words are being eroded at an alarming rate because so
many of today's communicators are ignorant and careless of *diction*. *Diction* is one of those words. If you tell a newspaper reporter
today that his diction is bad, he may reply that it doesn't matter
because he is not on radio or television. You will then explain that,
no matter what some of the new dictionaries say, diction has to do
with the choice of words, not the manner of pronouncing them,
and if *diction* is used to replace *enunciation,* then we are left without
a suitable replacement for *diction.* He may then say he is sorry, and
will try and do better.

Emulate may mean imitate, but there's more to it than that. To
emulate someone is to imitate him with the intent of rivalling or
excelling him, or, to put it colloquially, to try to beat him at his own
game. Rich Little does not emulate George Burns, he imitates him.
The misuse of this word is discussed further in Chapter 16.

Replica, properly used, means an exact copy of an artifact made
by the maker of the original. Those ships that sailed the ocean blue
in nineteen hundred and ninety-two were not replicas, they were
copies. This distinction is a lost cause, and is no longer supported
by lexicographers, but it is a good example of the unnecessary erosion of a word with a precise meaning. It has a nice sound to it —
much fancier than *copy* — so its precise meaning was wantonly destroyed by wide misuse.

I don't know how old the line is, but the first time I heard it, it was spoken by Liberace on television's *Tonight Show,* perhaps twenty or more years ago. The host (Johnny Carson or Jack Paar; I don't remember) had asked if Liberace had been troubled by some particularly scathing reviews of one of his concerts, and he said that, yes, he had been terribly upset.

"I cried all the way to the bank", he said.

To me, and to the studio audience, that was a delicious line. I don't suppose it was original then, but it was new to me, and that's what counts. And it did become an instant cliché, but in a peculiar way. In no time at all, everyone was saying "I *laughed* all the way to the bank". There's nothing funny about that.

When I was a lad we used to say "I couldn't care less". That somehow was a more emphatic statement than "I don't care". It was a useful bit of vernacular. Today's uninterested kids (and their parents, I guess) say "I *could* care less". If that means anything at all, it certainly doesn't mean what they're trying to say.

I don't know whether it's stupidity or perversity or a combination of the two that causes this sort of indifference to the meaning of words in catch-phrases. I don't understand people who apparently think they're quoting Shakespeare to good effect when they pluck out of context such phrases as "The play's the thing", or "Now is the winter of our discontent", and mouth them as though they mean something apt.

I was about to say that these are things that try my temper, and the thought came to mind that *temper* is a word ready to be added to the endangered species list. I hear people say "He has quite a temper". I don't know what that means. I usually assume they mean he is quick to fly off the handle, but that's not what they're saying. If they're saying anything, it's that he has a good temper.

The noun has a convoluted history that makes tedious reading in the *OED*, but, in the sense I'm talking about, what is important is the connotation of a balanced and salubrious mixture of qualities that leads to, among other things, resilience. So to lose one's temper is to become unbalanced. To have a bad temper is to be inclined that way.

Somehow, *temper* is becoming synonymous with *bad temper*. Instead of saying that someone has lost his temper, we may say that he's "showing his temper", and that is quite the opposite of what we mean. A person who loses his temper behaves badly, but a person who shows his temper behaves well.

However, in common usage, *a show of temper* now seems to mean a show of *bad* temper.

So it goes, with one word or expression after another. It's bad for everyone, but, if I may be permitted a slight show of self-pity, it's miserable for anyone who tries to communicate, especially by way of the mass media, for a living. The unbearable paradox is that the harder a writer tries to express himself with precision, the more likely he is to be misunderstood. If he seeks and finds the word that has the exact shade of meaning he wants to convey, there is an excellent chance that the word by now will have been so widely misused by his colleagues that he'll be lucky if one reader in a thousand grasps the nuance and if one in ten has even the vaguest idea what he means.

In such circumstances, it's all too easy (and I know, believe me!) to lapse into sloppiness, and that certainly doesn't help matters at all.

The news media are reporting an ever-increasing incidence of natural and unnatural events that make it desirable to *evacuate* the residents of a place.

I consider this an illogical use of *evacuate*, which means, simply, to make empty, but I can find little support for that opinion. The earliest (sixteenth century) findings listed in the *OED* have to do chiefly with bodily functions. Early in the seventeenth century, we find places being evacuated of inmates, but, at about the same time, we find inmates being evacuated, that is, removed. This makes no sense to me; evacuating a person suggests the preliminary work of the taxidermist. This simply indicates that writers of the twentieth century have no corner on illogicality, and that Sir Henry Wotton, author of the first *OED* sighting of this use, had he lived another three and a half centuries, would feel at home in a Canadian newsroom today, debilitating good words with the rest of them.

Both the *OED* and *Webster's II* put this use well down on the list, but neither suggests that there is anything improper about it. My faithful old *Webster's College*, however, recognizes only the uses I deem acceptable. One can never have too many dictionaries if one is on shaky ground when trying to bolster an argument.

I had a happier time seeking and failing to find support for the all-too-frequent modern use of *vault* as a transitive verb meaning suddenly elevate the position of someone, as in "Three birdies and an eagle on the back nine today *vaulted* him into third place". That is a use that Sir Henry wotted not of. "He vaulted into third place with..." would both correct the error and give the sentence more power.

The news media's passion for tight writing, mentioned earlier, leads to some ludicrous results. There are examples of this sprinkled throughout these pages, but since the misguided pursuit of tightness has an erosive effect, here's another one. A story on a meeting between a group of Metropolitan Toronto mayors and the Ontario government reported that "the mayors requested no more transfers of government departments outside Toronto". That was patently ridiculous. It suggests that the mayors had been requesting transfers, but now had stopped, and that the transfers in question had been from one smaller city to another. Actually, what the mayors requested was that the provincial government stop moving departments from Toronto to other places. Is that so difficult? Is that loose?

I have as much difficulty as anyone does in deciding what verb forms to use with collective nouns, but I think the problem can be dealt with more gracefully than it usually is. Here are some offences from print and TV:

"The news media has been negative...they don't provide a balanced view."

"A couple is seeking to regain custody of their children."

"General Motors unveils their 1987 models."

"The family is jubilant over their good fortune."

And so on. The writers of these sentences probably would argue that it is terribly difficult to figure out how to treat collectives, and they would be right. But it isn't all that difficult to be *consistent*, at least within the bounds of a single sentence or paragraph.

These examples, as do most such lapses, go from the singular to the plural or vice versa. It is not uncommon to hear a politician say "The government has their hands full", but, so far, I have been spared hearing "The government have its hands full". It is as though the speaker or writer is content with having decided that a collective should be treated as singular until he is faced with having to refer to a group of fellow humans as *it*.

There are guidelines that are of some help in dealing with this problem, but I doubt that they would be of much use to anyone unable to grasp the idea that having decided to treat a noun as singular, one should not change it to plural in the same breath, let alone in the same body of writing. Authorities allow the writer some discretion in the matter, but, of course, insist on consistency. Says Fowler:

But if the decision whether a noun of multitude is to be treated as a singular or as a plural is often a difficult business, and when ill made results at worst in a venial blemish, failure to abide by the choice when made, and plunging about between *it* and *they, have* and *has, its* and *their,* and the like, can only be called insults to the reader.

A writer who has grasped that point can then go a long way toward solving the problems presented by collectives, including nouns of multitude, by continuing to apply logic, which is often the only recourse. It makes sense to say "The committee *have* discussed the matter and *are* agreed", because we are referring to the actions of individuals. We do not mean that the committee as a whole discussed the matter (with someone else?). Logically, we would say "The committee *is* divided", because something must be a whole before it can be divided.

This approach is of limited help. One would not want to say "The committee are in agreement on extra billing but is divided on increasing fees". The solution is simply to say it another way: "The committee are agreed on extra billing but not on increasing fees."

Theodore Bernstein, ever pragmatic, suggests (in *The Careful Writer*):

> If the idea of oneness predominates, treat the noun as a singular. ("The number of accidents is larger this year" — because *number* is thought of as *total.*) If the idea of more-than-oneness predominates, treat the noun as a plural. ("A great number of accidents are preventable" — because *number* is equivalent to *many.*) With *number* or *total,* incidentally, a simple rule is possible: preceded by *the,* it is singular; preceded by *a,* it is plural.

There is lots to be said about the subject. There are lots of things to be said about it. I have just said one of them: *lots,* used colloquially to mean a great amount, should be treated as singular unless followed by *of* and a plural noun: "There *is* lots of wine, but there *aren't* lots of glasses."

Fowler, among many others, writes extensively on collectives, and gives many examples. I suggest reading him and remembering, if nothing else, his summing up, in which he says "In all these matters, good sense is the key... And it suggests a rule... Once you have made a proper choice, stay with it".

Erosion is particularly distressing to us older codgers who have spent a lifetime trying to learn a language that won't stand still. I'm not bothered at all to see the brilliantly innovative writing that is going on today — when I can find it. I object only to the much more easily found examples of stupid, ignorant, and careless disregard for the conventions that have enabled us for centuries to say some beautiful things to each other with some hope of being understood.

CHAPTER 15

English As She Is Spoke

Apart from a few ill-advised forays into radio and television, which I'd prefer to forget, my working life has been in the print media, so pronunciation has not been a vital consideration. I don't have a lot to say about it here. It has never bothered me to have my pronunciation corrected by someone more knowledgeable than I; in fact I appreciate it. However, I do know how to pronounce quite a few words — enough to make me sensitive to some of the gaffes made by professional talkers. I frequently growl back at the TV, pointing out to the guys with the blow-dried hair that there is no "you" in *bilingualism*, there is no "eh" in *lingerie*, there is no "ash" in *asphalt*, there is no "tea" in *consortium*, there is no "knock" in *Monaco*, and the like.

I don't get upset about sportscasters who feel compelled at times to talk about "DEEfence" and "OHfence". Things would be even more confusing if they didn't shift that emphasis to distinguish between the two when they come together in a rapid-fire commentary, but I hate hearing politicians, especially prime ministers, speak of our "DEEfence" policy or tax "REEform", and it bothers me a little to hear one of our Cabinet ministers pronouncing *route* as "rowt".

The dissolution of the Soviet Union, the Gulf War, the civil war in Yugoslavia, and many other events in this new age of instant worldwide television news have bombarded our ears with a profusion of tongue-twisting foreign place names. I'm sure it escapes nobody's notice that the pronunciation of these seems to depend entirely on the pronouncer. *Hercegovina* is a simple example. I have it on what I consider to be good authority (a Yugoslavian) that the accent is on the first syllable, but for months after the name began to appear in every newscast, most news readers emphasized the fourth syllable. (It was frequently transliterated as Herzegovina in the early days, but that's another topic.)

I have never understood our treatment of Chinese names. I remember *Beijing* being Peking and Peiping, but I don't know whether these are all the same name with new transliterations and/or pronunciations, or what. I know there has been much written on the subject, and I've read a little and comprehended none of it. I seem to recall the last major change, when I found out that *Deng* was to be pronounced "dung", and I could not see that as any great simplification.

The only reasonable way the average person can learn how foreign names are pronounced is by listening to radio and television. If newsreaders and on-air reporters can't agree on the pronunciation, what hope is there for the rest of us? It's not surprising, by the way, that announcers generally are more meticulous about pronunciation, since their job is to read words out loud while remembering which camera to look into, while the reporters do have other things to worry about.

The big networks have their own internal departments to provide their talkers with such guidance, and such services are also available one way or another to independent broadcasters. Obviously, these resources are not fully used, just as dictionaries are not adequately used in newspaper and magazine offices. It's a situation that is worth getting angry about.

The widespread attention being given the issue of sexual harassment in the workplace reached a peak during the televised Senate confirmation hearings of the U.S. Supreme Court nominee Clarence Thomas. There was an unfortunately ludicrous note lent to all the discussions and news reports by the fact that, while everyone was against such harassment, nobody was quite sure how to pronounce it.

Harass is correctly pronounced with the accent on the first syllable. (The same applies to *harassment* and *harassing.*) It rhymes with *embarrass.* No one has trouble pronouncing *embarrass* (although many have trouble spelling it). Most of the dictionaries I grew up with gave the first-syllable emphasis as the preferred pronunciation for *harass* and allowed the second-syllable stress as an alternative. Newer editions of the same dictionaries have reversed that order of preference, evidently bowing to the reality that practically no one was going to use the correct pronunciation anyway.

When the topic became all the rage, all the people before the cameras and microphones got into a blue funk about it. The amusing thing was not that one person would pronounce it one way or another but that the same person would pronounce it both ways, even in the same sentence. It did no one any good to "look it up in the dictionary", because dictionaries disagree with one another. As I suggested in Chapter 10, we are more and more poorly served by today's lexicographers.

CNN newsreaders, who are infrequently called on to deal with Canadian news, tend to call our provincial leaders "preMEERS", as in movie premieres. To give them the benefit of the doubt, which probably is a mistake, I assume they are familiar with *premier* as an adjective but not as a noun. I just wonder how long it will take for their pronunciation to catch on here.

It seems there are many young people today who think *southern* should be pronounced with a cry of pain in the first syllable. This is perhaps understandable in light of the correct pronunciation of *south,* but one would expect weather forecasters, of all people, to know better. One would be wrong. I have heard it mispronounced by many of the current crop of TV weatherpersons. Since I don't trust weatherpersons even in the matter of weather forecasts, I am not likely to turn to them for guidance in elocution, but there are impressionable young people out there. Also, there are newscasters to be found who need to be told that *Gloucester* rhymes with Mr. Foster, not ouster.

Broadcasters who pompously say "consorteeum" are laughable. Ordinary people who say "consorshyum" are correct. But what are we to make of the editor of the *Oxford American Dictionary,* who, on a television talk show, pronounced *exiguous* with a soft G? Whom can you trust?

Natives of some parts of the United States, particularly Texas, have difficulty pronouncing the short E. CBS News star Dan Rather, a Texan, has publicly admitted to having had to cope with that, but he has been pretty successful at it. One who has not been is CNN's Dave Walker, who keeps hitting us with such lines as "The bill is supported by Minnie in the synod", or "Tin workers walked off the job" when actually it was ten workers. How come some of these guys can pronounce *Texas,* but say "cintral" Texas?

The thought has occurred to me that at least some of the people who say *averted* for *avoided* might have been raised in Brooklyn.

I heard the U.S. Senator Joseph Biden say "docTRYnal". You may recall that he is not noted for the originality of his speeches, but he frequently does display originality in both diction and pronunciation.

There is plenty of room for argument on the subject of whether English speakers should attempt to pronounce foreign names with a foreign accent. Nobody here is ever criticized for not giving *Mexico* its Spanish pronunciation, but TV reporters get slammed for saying "Nicaragyoua". Americans (and even some Canadians, who ought to know better) thought during the 1992 Winter Olympics that by simply leaving the T out of *Albertville* they were giving it the French pronunciation. This is a can of worms I occasionally peek into, but have no intention of opening now or possibly ever.

On the day the Gulf War ended, I was musing about what I would do with my fortune if I could have a small unit of currency for every time I heard the non-words "jubulant", "jubulation", and even (God help us) "jubulance" spoken on the various TV news broadcasts I spent much of the day watching. Still, it was a change from hearing about wars that were "esculating".

As I said in the beginning, this is not my favourite subject, but I can't leave it without mentioning that there is no such thing as a "chaise lounge" and that a "Cretan" probably is not a cretin.

CHAPTER 16

The Scribe *Sans* Quill or Quire

I am able to recall the dates of just three crucial points in my adult working life. I have never been able to cope with historically significant dates. I know 55 B.C., and 1066 A.D., and 1867 A.D. all mean something to Canadian WASPs, and that's about it. It helps. Everything of consequence happened either before or after or between one or more of those dates, and that applies also to my own turning points.

First there was January 26, 1948, when I retired as a toy salesman for Eaton's and moved from Montreal to Ottawa to report for my first newspaper job. On December 31, 1960, I moved to Toronto to begin work as a columnist for *The Toronto Star*. That first relationship with the *Star* lasted five months, but I have remained a Torontonian these thirty years and more. The events of my adult life are catalogued in my memory as occurring either before or after that move.

Finally, there was October 15, 1982, when I bought my first computer. My address remained the same, and so did my work as a freelance writer. This milestone involved no change of address, merely a change of life. I'm not sure it was for the better, but it was drastic.

Replacing the typewriter with the computer as the primary mechanical tool of the writer's trade is a vastly more traumatic change than the move from the quill pen to the typewriter, although I can recall reading, in earlier times, a number of essays by writers who felt their work had suffered from the latter transition.

For better or for worse, the computer revolution has changed the business of writing. Employees of newspapers and magazines had no choice. Freelance writers did, and many of the very best have opted to stick with the typewriter. Such conservatism is common in the profession. When I joined *The Ottawa Journal,* the founding publisher, the venerable P.D. Ross, was still alive and working and refusing to use a typewriter. His pencilled editorials were the dread of the composing room. The linotype operators had a sixth sense that warned them of the arrival of any piece of copy from him, and there would be a mad scramble for the washroom. It may be that his writing would have been adversely affected had he used a typewriter, but certainly the process of getting his thoughts into print would have been streamlined.

There is no question that the switch from typewriters to word-processing computers has a similar but even greater streamlining effect on that process, but there is still plenty of argument about the effect of the new technology on the quality of the output of those who use it. That argument is outside the scope of this book, but it *is* relevant to suggest that the technology has the potential to mitigate many of the sins chronicled herein.

I have to confess that there have been occasions when I have looked at a page of my own typewritten copy into which I had pencilled every emendation there was room for, found I would like to make one more change, and said the hell with it — I haven't got the time or energy to retype the whole page and it'll have to go as is. That excuse is gone forever. With a word processor, you can go on editing *ad infinitum* and still produce clean text. The other side of that coin is that there comes a time to quit and tell yourself that this is as good as it's going to get. The ease of electronic editing often will carry one past that point.

There are various aids built into word processors. The most common is called a spell-checker (alas, not a spelling checker). This is simply a device that checks every word you type against a list of many thousands of (presumably) correctly spelled words. It can be applied to a finished piece of text, or be set to beep at you the instant you type a word it doesn't recognize. It can be of some use to the writer who recognizes its limitations, but it will not, for example, warn you that you have written *there* instead of *their* (one of the commonest mistakes made by non-professional writers and not a few professionals).

Another common adjunct to the word processor is the grammar checker. (I have seen an advertisement for such a product that called it a "grammer" checker. No kidding. A spelling checker would have caught that one.) These are pretty primitive, but can be of help to the non-writer who is forced by some circumstance to try to express himself in writing. They simply get in the way of any moderately competent writer, but they have come a long way in a very few years. Even now they can catch certain errors that often slip past experienced writers, such as the failure to close an open quotation or parenthesis.

I have something truly useful in the innards of my own computer: a dictionary. It is a far cry from the *OED* (which is available in computer form at a price far beyond my reach), but it is a serviceable electronic version of the sort of desk dictionary most people like to keep in reach. It enables me to stop typing in the middle of a word and have the definition of that word before my eyes in five seconds, and mine is by no means the fastest home computer available. I consider it a good investment. It would be of no use to writers who consider it infra dig to consult a dictionary at all, but could be a boon to those who would look something up if it didn't take so much effort.

Computers, then, do have the potential to help in the fight against linguistic anarchy, but only if writers and editors care enough to use them.

There are negative aspects to the computer as a writing tool. One of them is the enticement to become hooked on the many marvellous advantages it offers and then have the thing break down just when you need it most. I used to refer to my first computer system as my $5,000 pencil. But if you break the point of a pencil, it isn't too difficult to sharpen it, and if you're careful you might not even cut yourself. Nothing much ever went wrong with any of the old Underwood Standard typewriters I used and loved for decades. When anything did it was never much of a problem to find another one and switch to it. Typing on a computer isn't all that different; it's the other features that matter. Apart from being able to edit without retyping, one of the most valuable of these is the ability to search through piles of files for specific information and then to "cut-and-paste" the results of that search into the text you're writing.

Computer users tend to program their systems to make various features even easier to use. Thereby they dig more traps for themselves. Eventually they reach a point at which a computer breakdown is a disaster. You can't resharpen a broken computer, or just replace the ribbon, or even switch to another machine unless it's programmed the same way your regular one is. Believe me. I've been there. This adds a lot of tension when you're facing a deadline.

The day I got that first computer, I broke my oath never to use *access* as a verb. Almost overnight, I stopped making derisive references to *computer jargon* and began respectfully calling it *terminology,* which, of course, is what it is. Jargon is what *others* use. Terminology is what I and my fellow computer users use.

Computer terminology is also called *computerese*, particularly by those who don't speak it, and that term will serve us here. Whatever you call it, it is a young and imperfect language. This is not surprising, considering that the generation that is developing it is also hell-bent on destroying English. Computer enthusiasts will tell you, rightly, that they must use computerese in order to understand one another. In view of this, it seems odd that many of them show no sign of having the same feeling about English. Few of them worry about whether *presently* means now or means soon. Few care that there is a distinction between *incredible* and *incredulous*. It is inevitable that a technical vocabulary created by people with no regard for precise diction in their use of the mother tongue will be a mess.

The computerese verb *access* is one of the least offensive neologisms. It simply means to gain access to. A computer user might ask you if he may access your bathroom (you should refuse), but he is unlikely to. When he is using his computer, however, he does so damn' much accessing that a short verb is essential. *Access* serves the purpose well, and such use is harmless if it is not permitted to escape to the outside world.

Not so pardonable is the computerese corruption of *clone*. I have what is commonly (and unfortunately) called an IBM clone. This is a misnomer. In English, a clone is an organism that is genetically identical to its forebear, and the word is not a good choice to describe an imitation. Before *clone* gained currency in computerese, some manufacturers used *workalike* for this purpose. That made more sense, but I suppose three syllables were a bit much for some people.

My printer, the manual tells me, "emulates" two standard makes of printer. It may, indeed, do so, since *emulate* means rival, but for years writers of computerese have been misusing *emulate* to mean "simulate", and I am certain the writer of this manual meant *simulate*. I once raised this question with an extremely competent programmer of broad interests and wide education, who carefully explained to me what *emulate* means in computerese, and I had to say again that I knew all that, but was complaining that the word was a bad choice in the first place. *Emulate* has the particular connotation of rivalling and attempting to better. There are many products on the market whose makers would like to have you think they emulate better-known brands, but most of them merely simulate them.

One of the main action keys on a computer keyboard is labelled either ENTER or RETURN. What it does is "enter" what you've just typed into the innards of the beast. It doesn't "return" anything. Somewhere along the way, some bigbrain had the idea that, because in some circumstances the ENTER key does something that resembles the function performed by the carriage return key on an electric typewriter, people new to computers would find the keyboard friendlier if the key were labelled RETURN. Millions of computers, including the Apple, adopted that aberration, and the resultant confusion during conversations between users of different brands was terrible to behold. It almost destroyed one of my oldest friendships. I was merely trying to help, but after telling him a few thousand times that when I said "enter" I meant that he should hit his stupid RETURN key, I began to scream. I do believe that today there are ever fewer ENTER keys labelled RETURN, praise be.

Computerese is as much abused as is English. Many, perhaps most, who try to speak it fail to grasp the distinction between *bug* (a software problem) and *glitch* (a hardware problem), or between *upload* and *download.*

I'm particularly fascinated by the trouble computer users have with the latter pair of terms. They refer to the transfer of files from one computer system to another. In general, if you are uploading a file you are sending (or transmitting) it to another computer; if you are downloading it, you are receiving it from another computer, but that's oversimplifying things. *Send* and *receive* are not adequate to indicate which end is passive and which is active. If you call my computer and send me a file, you are on the active end. You are uploading the file, and my computer is receiving it — passively — not downloading it. If you instruct my computer to send you a file, my computer will send it — not upload it. You are still calling the shot, so you are downloading.

To put it another way, if I have a file for you, I might call your computer and upload it, to you, or you might call mine and download it. Either way, my computer is sending and yours is receiving, but *upload* or *download* is required to indicate which end is controlling the action. I find this a hell of a lot easier to understand than to explain, but I just wanted to make the point that I have run into many computer users who have been performing these operations practically every day for years, and they still say one when they mean the other. I have no idea why they find this so difficult, but the resulting confusion, while not terribly serious, is damnably annoying.

Some of my friends who are "into" computers tell me that you can't discuss the subject without saying *interface*. I have a computer glossary that defines interface as "that which connects one thing to another thing". What ever happened to *connector*? But never mind that. What are we to do with the police consultant who wrote "Constables will be expected to interface with the various minorities"? We don't need *interface* as a noun, let alone as a verb, in general usage.

I am not at all fluent in computerese. I came to it late in life, and am still too preoccupied with my effort to learn English to do well with a second language, but I have observed that the people who speak it well are those who speak English well. The personal computer phenomenon is little more than a dozen years old, and the lingo it spawned has made only minor inroads in English, but this will change. What it has done so far is surely far less frightening than the fact that we now seem to have a suffix — -*gate* — that means scandal. Computerese, which is being created by people whose lack of regard for English is exceeded only by their ignorance of it, has, so far, done nothing as bloody awful as that to us, but it will, it will. On the plus side, like English, it is graced by vigorous slang. I love *farkle* and *kludge* and *munge*, to name just a few, and some of the jargon tickles me. A devotee of computer communications might say "Yeah, I know Fred. We've never eyeballed, but we've keyboarded, and I've voiced him the odd time".

Acronyms and abbreviations proliferate in the world of computer users. This is normal among professionals in any field, but is intensified by the number of hobbyists and "end-users" in computing. Many terms are used without real comprehension, and the result is a microcosm of the general linguistic chaos. In the real world, many acronyms are widely used and understood in the manner of words, even though the writer or reader or speaker cannot correctly quote the title the abbreviation represents, any more than I could give you the etymology of most of the words I use.

A good example of the overnight corruption of a word at the hands of the news media is the sad story of *hacker*. Not long ago, a hacker was an expert computer user who could modify hardware or the software code that controlled it. When a few hackers went bad and started doing harm, the press grabbed the word and turned it into a pejorative. One day it was an honour to be called a hacker. The next day it implied criminality. This was upsetting to a lot of honest, self-respecting people, and it led to a lot of justifiable press-bashing among computists.

Two things struck me almost as soon as I started using a computer. One was the relative ease of editing copy — my own or anyone else's

— with a word processor. The other was the capability of transferring great quantities of verbiage over great distances. Combining these features, I reasoned, should make it possible to start a modest enterprise. I would offer copy-editing services to business people who were not writers but who had to write. They would write their memos, or sales letters, or brochures, or whatever on their word processors, then transmit the documents to me via ordinary phone lines. I would make changes that would save them from serious misunderstandings or the embarrassment of revealing their inadequate grasp of English, and transmit the emended copy back to them, probably within the hour for small jobs.

Although I thought I couldn't miss, I did. I had overlooked a few important truths, the most fundamental of which was that the people I wanted to sell the service to were ignorant of the fact that they needed it. The more they needed it, the less likely they were to realize it. Another was that they didn't know how to use their computers.

I did get some business of this sort, and it was discouraging to take a document of, say, a couple of thousand words, make perhaps a hundred corrections in spelling, punctuation, grammar, and so on, and then be told "But you didn't even *change* anything". I didn't bring up this subject to grind an axe. It seems to me a sorry state of affairs when people trying to make a buck by communicating with others haven't the foggiest notion how sloppily they're expressing themselves.

CHAPTER 17

Vox Populi ad Absurdum

I made reference in the first chapter to electronic bulletin board services (BBSs) for computer users. This is a phenomenon of the fourth quarter of the twentieth century that cries out for the attention of social historians. There may be perceptive books about it, but I am not aware of any. It came to my attention in 1982, when I first laid hands on a home computer. A decade later, I am still staggered by its implications — and its ironies.

I've found that trying to convey the idea of this form of computer communication to anyone who has no hands-on experience of it ranges from difficult to impossible, but I keep trying.

People all over the world, literally, are talking among themselves by this means. There is a vast, unruly, almost anarchic grid of interconnected networks moving many tens of thousands of messages among hundreds of thousands of individuals every day, and I may be counting in inadequate units. The grid is so sprawling and undisciplined that even the people deeply involved in its operation can't quite grasp its scope. There has never been any means of communication remotely like it. Radio and television reach millions, even billions, of people, but those people can't reach back. With far

less effort than it takes to scribble and mail a postcard to one person, I can type and send a message that is available in minutes to a
potential audience of thousands of people. The thought that stag-
gers the imagination is that any or all of them can reply just as
quickly. Fortunately, relatively few of them do.

There's something nightmarish about all this. One way I've
tried to describe it is in terms of radio phone-in shows, which I am
not fond of. I've never bought the idea that any idiot with access to
a telephone is entitled to a huge audience. Now, imagine, if you can,
a phone-in show *without a host or moderator.* Think about it.

A couple of years ago, I had some correspondence with a chap in
Norway. He was not a writer, and he was not fluent in English, but
he had little trouble getting information and ideas across. His messages were, well, *quaint* comes to mind, and I enjoyed reading
them. He was a bit apologetic about his English. I wrote him once
to the effect that I found his writing easier to understand than that
of many products of our own school system. I meant it. He obviously had some good grounding, whether from a school or by self-
teaching, and, above all, he was *trying.* For whatever reason, it was
important to him to learn the language, and he was going great
guns.

The majority of English-speaking people I've come across in
this way are far less interested in learning the language than he was.
Possibly that's because they think they already know it. After all, it's
their native tongue, and they've been to school. I have been
appalled by the degree of arrogance displayed by many such people,
especially young people, who don't know that some of us know that
our schools are in the business of graduating students who may or
may not be literate.

One has to be careful about judging people on the basis of what
they write for public consumption in this medium. Allowances

have to be made for those whose first language is not English and for those who have special problems. We don't see or hear these writers, and tend to make decisions about them purely on the basis of what we see of their writing. I've had quite a bit of correspondence with a brilliant fellow who cannot speak, hear, or see, but he can pound a keyboard, and I'm not about to jump on him for misplacing a modifier. It's also difficult to guess a writer's age. I have many times been inclined to forgive someone's writing in the belief that I am corresponding with, perhaps, a fourteen-year-old, only to discover eventually that it's a middle-aged person.

It also has to be noted that there is no way of determining just what sort of cross-section you're being exposed to. The people who use this means of communication have one thing in common: they have access to a computer. That places them in a minority, albeit a significant one, and suggests that they might enjoy educational advantages over the less privileged.

What is relevant here is that the BBS medium reveals not only a widespread inability to use English as a means of communication but also a widespread ignorance of that inability, and, in consequence, a lack of interest in doing anything about it.

The ease of getting into the medium has had an unfortunate result. Before all this, anyone who wanted to express a thought to a significant number of people had to go to considerable effort — hire a hall and lure a crowd in, persuade an editor to publish his work, buy or rent a printing press, or whatever. Now, people can sit down at a computer console and blather away to hundreds or thousands of victims to their hearts' content.

An interesting phenomenon became a tradition almost overnight when large numbers of people began using this medium. Those with hard-earned knowledge of the new technology displayed a remarkable willingness to share their expertise with novices, and this willingness to help spread into every area of special interest. (An unfortunate side-development was the excessive willingness of participants to share misinformation just to get into the act. People remain people, whether they own computers or not.)

A very large part of the public message traffic among these systems involves the quest for information. A caller will post a message to "ALL", asking for specific information or advice — where to buy something, how to fix something, what is the significance of a new income tax regulation, how to de-flea a hamster, who was our fifth prime minister...literally anything you can think of. Almost always, such messages will receive a number of replies, some of which are likely to be useful. The depressing thing about it all is that the majority of the queries and replies are so badly written that the usefulness of the medium is severely hampered. I don't know how many times I have written something like "Thanks for your reply, but perhaps I didn't phrase my question clearly. What I was asking was..." I am, of course, usually lying, because my query *was* clearly expressed, but one must be polite and acknowledge well-meant attempts to help. If one replies snappishly or not at all, one is less likely to hear from someone who does understand and does have an answer.

There is a three-element problem here.

What we have is a great tangled mass of communications — confusion confounded simply because (1) many, if not most, people don't know how to state a problem; (2) even if a problem *is* stated clearly, many, if not most, people will misread it; and (3) even if the question is understood, many, if not most, people are unable to word a reply clearly.

Virtually every BBS I've looked into in the decade since I discovered the medium, ranging from the tiny one I ran on my own computer to the vast CompuServe system, has provided electronic conferences for writers. That excited me, in the beginning, but not for long. I still check them out occasionally, and things haven't changed. Some of them are visited by professional, although not eminent, writers who, for the most part, are eager to discuss almost anything but writing. For the rest of it, the conferences are populated mainly by young people who are eager for advice on how to become writers without working at it.

I've lost count of the number of messages I've seen from these ambitious young folk saying that they have read a lot of "Hemmingway" and admire him greatly. Hemingway himself was a bit careless with his spelling, and might have accepted the admiration of would-be writers who wouldn't take the trouble to spell his name correctly, but I refuse to take them seriously. These wannabes, as they are sometimes called, nurture wild dreams of fame and fortune accruing to them from their semiliterate outpourings of stream-of-consciousness babble. They have no interest in trying to learn the craft they think they want to practise, and they're a blight on the BBS scene.

Protocol is not a word that is on everyone's lips most of the time. Primarily it is used in reference to the customs and regulations dealing with diplomatic formality, precedence, and etiquette.

To those involved in computer communications, it has a special and important meaning. For any computer to communicate with one or more other computers, be it in an office network, in direct communication between two machines, in a connection with an electronic mail service, in using a remote database service, in calling a BBS, or whatever else, there must be agreement on both ends as to which of certain technical standards are being used. This is called *protocol,* and if two computers are using different protocols, they can't communicate with one another. If you read anything about computer communications, you'll see this word over and over again.

People who use this form of communication are using the written, not the spoken, word. You might, then, expect that most of them would know how to spell *protocol,* right? Wrong. It is one of the most frequently misspelled words in computer jargon. In BBS messages, it is probably misspelled more often than not. I've seen "protacol", "protocal", "protocall", and probably every other variation you could dream up, so often that I barely notice any more. It's as bizarre as reading a cookbook that tells you to "boyle" this and "baik" that and "sotay" the other thing. The word *cache* has a special technical meaning for computer users, but a remarkable number of them write "cash". I suppose that reveals what their priorities are.

Here are a couple of excerpts from just one example (chosen almost at random from hundreds of possible ones) of an effort at communication by a product of the Ontario school system:

> Over the years I have found that NDP voters are simply misinformed, as you seem to be. Tories and Liberals inexperienced? Wrong, when I say inexperience I mean the 78% of the entire NDP party have never beenelected before, some have never even run before, and past parties usually have a rate some where around 20% if not lower. This inexperienced is very dangerous because it is like putting any group off the street and expect them to run a province.

> Re: solutions — Giving solutions like the NDP is easy but giving thought-out solutions that actually work is harder. (eg. of NDP solution — spend 9.7 billion and pass the check to next goverment and tax payers). Ressessions work themselves free. Soon people get of saving and start to spend. If you do not believe me look at the last ressission.

In my belief goverments are there to keep law and order and help the injured or mentally retarted, help those finacially those who have lost their jobs temporiarly, provide free health care to those who can not afford it. Above all I believe that people should be allowed to become as successful as he or she wants to be and then choose what he would like to do with his money instead of what the goverments choose to do with his money. I believe that goverments should balance the budget as much as possible.

What is amazing about these passages is not that the writer intended the message to be taken seriously, but that it actually was. Several people responded more or less thoughtfully, and the discussion went on until those who responded got tired of trying to get anything across to the writer. We also have here a powerful bit of support for the theory that a weak grasp of one's native language is detrimental not only to communication but to thought.

There are age-old jokes, frequently encouraged by pharmacists, about the illegible writing of doctors. Having now seen, via computer networks, many legible communications from members of the medical profession, I think I know why they prefer their characteristic illegible scrawls. If you can't read their handwriting, you won't notice that they can't write plain English. I once got a prescription from a doctor who was careless enough to write it clearly enough for me to decipher it, and the first thing I noticed was that he could not spell the name of the drug he was prescribing. Filled me with confidence. I have saved and enshrined a prescription that reads ONE TEASPOONFUL EVERY 4 HOURS WHEN NECESSARY FOR COUGH AFTER MEALS. I actually think I might know what that means, and am comforted somewhat by the realization that misinterpreting it would probably not be fatal.

As I have said more than once here, I recognize that there is more to leading a productive and useful life than the use of good English, but, dammit, it makes me nervous reading some of the medical conferences on the computer networks. I don't look there for prose of classic elegance. I merely want to be assured that these guys are able to communicate effectively with each other (even if not with their patients). Certainly some of them are, but serious deficiencies in reading and writing skills are demonstrated by enough of them to give me a severe case of jitters.

A revealing custom has sprung up among BBS users, who use *emoticons* to aid them in overcoming the lack of voice inflection, facial expression, and body language in this form of communication. The first one of these I noticed was a simple -) used to identify a tongue-in-cheek remark. More elaborate ones evolved, most of which have to be looked at with one's head cocked to the left. Thus :-) is a smiling face, or "smiley". There are now dozens of variations indicating frowns, expressions of disgust or bemusement, raised eyebrows, and whatnot. There are even lexicons available for people who are more interested in these than I am.

This development suggests a couple of conclusions. One is that the majority of its users regard electronic messaging as a form of idle conversation rather than the means of rapid exchange of written communication that it is. With this in mind, it is easier to understand the excessive sloppiness characteristic of BBS messages. Also, it's clear that the users are not at all comfortable with the written word and have a real need for such crutches. Some scorn emoticons, putting them in the "nudge-nudge-wink-wink" category. But the BBS enthusiast who eschews their use runs the risk of having to write many messages reading something like: "I was only kidding, for God's sake. Loosen up." Thousands of such messages flood the networks every day.

One can never be quite sure that one's leg is not being pulled. A message containing the following line stopped me in my tracks: "I always suggest following this rule, like I did when I was teaching English." I'm still not entirely sure that it wasn't meant humorously, but after reading quite a bit of correspondence from the same man, I became convinced that it was no joke.

CHAPTER 18

Word Games

I don't have a lot to say about word games. I don't much like them now. Over the years they got to seem more and more like work. But they were once important to me, and I'd like to point out how much they can contribute to overcoming some of the linguistic ailments that plague our times.

When I was a young reporter, my friends were my colleagues. Social life was business life in more amiable surroundings. We worked together through a six-day (sometimes seven-day) week of very long days, goofing off as much as possible, since the only way to get any drinking time was to steal it. There would be a party at one of our homes virtually every Saturday night, and, inevitably, we would play word games. I don't know if this goes on any more, and I'm not sure that it matters. It indicates that the people in those circles then were interested in our language, and I think this fooling around helped us all to use it better.

I made it through only one year of high-school Latin, and I made it because the teacher knew some neat Latin word games. Perhaps I didn't learn much, but I absorbed a fair amount of vocabulary and a sudden awareness of how much Latin had to do with English. I have since wished that a similar experience with Greek had been forced on me.

Word games are Good Things. There is evidence of their existence more than two millennia ago. People, even people who consider any serious effort to learn English a drag, like them. The most popular TV game show of recent years has been *Wheel of Fortune,* which evolved from the first word game I ever learned: Hangman. Kids used to play it on paper; now you can play it on a computer, and I do. I hope my grandchildren will. One of the most successful TV game shows of the 1960s was *Password,* another word game that people could and did (and still do) play at home and at parties and in bars with no more equipment than some pencils and a few scraps of paper. Scrabble, a home game that does require some equipment, has been a huge moneymaker for decades.

I had a long-time friend who was a successful writer for radio and TV for many years. He had a yen to move into print, but felt he would have to make a drastic improvement in his spelling skills, which had atrophied over the years, so he took up the solving of crossword puzzles as an enjoyable means of doing so. It worked well for him, and had an unexpected side-effect. When he tired a little of the standard form, he discovered, and became hooked on, cryptic crosswords. Like most addicts, he felt compelled to proselytize, and I was an easy mark. He then got a yen to try writing his own, and dragged me along. He thought it was fun. I wasn't so sure it was *that* much fun, but thought it might be profitable, especially since Canadian-made puzzles of this genre were in short supply. The upshot was an outpouring of about 900 published cryptics, written by one or the other or both of us, 750 of them published by *The Toronto Star* under the logo "The Star Cryptic". My friend's name was David Harriman. His career ended early in 1987 when that indiscriminate reaper, cancer, cut him down in his prime. Mine stopped early in 1991, when I simply ran dry.

This involvement with cryptic crosswords, which came rather late in life for me, was an educational experience. The original idea was fun, and the later idea was money. The education part was incidental, but it was there. I realize that this particular crossword genre is a mystery to most people. I don't want to get into much explanation, but the general idea is to give the solver the necessary information while using every possible trick to conceal it. Probably no language in the world is better suited to this purpose than English. It has a huge vocabulary, an abundance of homonyms, homophones, synonyms, antonyms, weird spellings, syntactical oddities, and ambiguities. It is a damnably difficult language that might have been designed for the express purpose of confusing people, and that's what the game is all about.

I wouldn't suggest that anyone look to cryptics for an education. They are simply fun, but those who become addicted will learn to take a different and more critical attitude toward everything they read or write or hear or say, and that's not a Bad Thing.

Limericks are more a form of wordplay than of poetry. These bits of formally constructed doggerel seem to have an irresistible appeal for casual poetasters. They lend themselves to trick rhymes (and to vulgarity), and their construction is a harmless pursuit. The limerick is an art form, but one that appears to be ridiculously simple to people who are looking for an art form to dabble in. I've seen hundreds of attempts at limerick writing by wannabes who can barely spell their own names correctly, and the results are atrocious, showing that their authors have absolutely no concept of the metrical and rhyming rules.

But there are many great ones, and there have been huge and scholarly collections of them published.

There is a particular form, called the post-office limerick, that has been cruelly damaged by progress. Here is an old example:

> A bookworm from York Harbor, Me.
> Found pleasure in reading Monte.
> He got little wallop
> From Miss Winsor's trollop
> And Finnegan's Wake caused him pe.

If you've got that figured out, you can see how changes in postal codes have hit the genre pretty hard. There was another one, which I can't fully recall, that depended on *Fla.* being the abbreviation for Florida, and on *CA not* being the abbreviation for California. The bloody postal service bureaucrats just charged ahead with no thought for the damage they were doing to a great literary form.

CHAPTER 19

A Grab-bag of Eyewhackers

It has bothered me from time to time that the tone in these pages is almost entirely negative, when, in fact, there is so much Canadian writing that I enjoy and admire, but the purpose has been to draw attention to the other side of the coin, and I can't stop now.

I was discussing the sorry state of book editing in Canada with someone on the fringes of the publishing business a few years ago, and mentioned a Canadian novel I had read recently. It was an "action thriller" that had a lot to be said in its favour. But, I said, it had been spoiled for me by the fact that at least once on almost every page, I had been eyewhacked by some major or minor error that should have been caught, if not by the author, then by a diligent editor. I emphasized that I was not exaggerating the frequency of the errors. He pressed me for an example ("Give me one, just one, example"), and I regretted not having the book at hand, because it would have been a delight to leaf through a bit of it, pointing out one blunder after another. Relying on memory, I mentioned something that had tickled me — a reference to the twelve-foot-square trunk of a car. I said I was prepared to believe that the car had a twelve-square-foot trunk, but that a twelve-foot-square one would make for a rather ludicrous (and in fact illegal) family sedan.

"Oh, well, for heaven's sake", he pooh-poohed, "that's a slip *anyone* could make."

I don't remember my reply to that. I try to block out all recollection of my rare moments of rudeness. *Of course* it's a slip anyone could make, but I, for one, find little pleasure in reading a book containing hundreds of slips anyone could make.

It is quite common in arguments for one person to demand a specific example and then dismiss the one that is given. It was for that reason that I set out to stock up on examples to include here, in the hope that they would add up to more than could easily be shrugged off. I am going to conclude with a grab-bag of gaffes from my collection, some of which are without comment because I hope no comment is necessary, and some of which are elaborated on just because I felt like elaborating on them. Some of them go back a few years, but that doesn't mean they aren't still being committed.

A newscaster fondly remembered the late Mae West for "all the double-meaning entendre".

Bashing is enjoying a vogue in journalism these days, as in *gay-bashing, cop-bashing, tenant-bashing,* or, for that matter, *press-bashing.* It's a colourful colloquialism, and I have no objection to its use in the popular press. But when a political reporter referred to "federal-bashing", he was language-bashing. The term calls for a noun; *federal* is an adjective (although *Federal* does have a very limited use as a noun). If the writer wanted to be properly slangy, he should have said *fed-bashing.* Perhaps he felt that would be undignified.

We sometimes are told of a "contentious debate" in Parliament. I don't know of any other kind.

A reporter said that "the prime minister had no reaction". The PM may not have expressed one, but surely it is a bit presumptuous of the reporter to say that he had none.

When the pre-Mulroney Tories ended a lengthy boycott of Parliament, we were told that the next step was "to cut the energy bill down to mutually digestible chunks". That would mean that the chunks could digest each other. There is no saving that sentence. The man who wrote it should be sent out to a bread-and-water dinner with the police reporter who wrote "So far, any leads in the investigation have come up empty".

A CNN reporter said someone had "culled through a huge amount of research". *Cull* means select. Do you select *through* anything? I don't. We continually hear of police and jurists and such "sifting through masses of evidence". Again, why *through*? Do you sift through flour? No, you sift flour through a sieve.

A TV news report showed rescue workers "scurrying survivors to waiting ambulances". The last time I looked, *scurry* was not a transitive verb. Probably the next time I look, it will be.

Police no longer investigate an accident to find what caused it, they "investigate the cause". I do not understand how you can investigate something if you don't know what it is, but I suppose the police have powers the rest of us lack. These would be the same police, I guess, who are always said to "have no motive for the crime". Why should we expect them to have a motive for a crime they didn't commit?

It has become common to hear and read that someone has been forbidden *from* doing something rather than forbidden *to* do it. The CBC reported that Mikhail Gorbachev had been "banned from leaving the country". You don't ban someone from doing something. He was forbidden to leave the country. Someone may have simply misread *barred*, but I wouldn't bet on it.

One comes to expect solecisms from television, but not from *Time*, which used to be one of the most meticulously edited magazines anywhere. Thomas Griffith, in his *Time* magazine column "Newswatch", produced this sentence: "So, in the weeks before Reagan began his *real* vacation in Santa Barbara, his press aides have been busy arranging symbolic non-news and photo opportunities to show a caring and involved president." What was needed there was a caring and involved editor to watch the watcher and straighten out those verbs.

Another little goof spotted in *Time* was in a story about an effort by the British Broadcasting Corporation to get into the Asian market: "Their satellite channel...is reaching 38 Asian countries that number half the world's population. But only about half a million households actually own satellites." The use of *satellite* to describe a dish antenna designed to receive TV signals relayed by satellites is foolish, but it's catching on.

Here are two more journalistic gems: "Many are blaming Marcos with manipulating the votes", and "Debris rained down from the sky, similar to what happened with Challenger". There is no hope for these sentences. You don't blame Marcos *with* something. You blame him *for* it. But *blame* is wrong here, anyway. It should have been either *accused him of* or *charged him with*. The other example needs no comment.

When a witness to a riot at a rock concert tells a Toronto TV newsman that "I seen this bunch of people laying there", we merely assume the young man to be the unfortunate product of the Ontario school system. But when the newsman replies "They must of ran out of things to throw", we might change our minds and decide that the young man's problem is that he has been listening too closely to TV newsmen. (The *laying* part of the quote is dealt with elsewhere.)

Referring to the investigation of a terrible explosion in Texas, an NBC newsman told us that "officials are attempting to re-create the disaster", inspiring in us the fervent hope that the characteristic inefficiency of officialdom would prevail.

A reporter for Ontario's Global-TV network informed us that something had been "eroded away", leaving us to hope that, with any luck, it might someday be eroded back into being.

Reporting on a breakdown of salary negotiations, a Toronto radio announcer said that Metropolitan Toronto police had voted "to carry out their promised threat of a work-to-rule campaign". Well, of course, you can promise to make a threat, but you can't carry out the threat until you've kept your promise, and, anyway, that one is too ridiculous to even play with.

One who did not say what he meant a few years back was the wire-service writer who explained that the Canadian proposal for patriation of the constitution would have to be presented to the British Parliament, "which legally must approve the measure". Perhaps most of us know he meant that the measure, to become law, required the approval of the British Parliament, but what he said, in effect, was that the British Parliament is required by law to approve the measure, whether it wants to or not, and that was not true.

At the time of the unsuccessful attempt to rescue the American hostages in Iran, a TV newsman in Toronto said that "Canada was not told of the abortive rescue attempt in advance". Was he supposing that the U.S. knew in advance that the mission would prove abortive?

A *Globe and Mail* "Quote of the Day", attributed to the chairman of the colleges committee of the Ontario Federation of Students: "English is a fundamental thing. And, like, everybody should have a good level of it."

What's all this we read about "preventative medicine"? Is that something designed to preventate illnessness?

What did the reporter at a hotel fire mean by saying "An estimate of the damage is unknown at this time"?

Who is going around scaring the daylights out of doors? I see signs everywhere saying such things as "For emergency use only. This door is alarmed".

CNN promotion writers were bragging in 1991 about the news network's having won a 1992 Ace Award for its "unprecedented live coverage of the Gulf war". Since there is no way there could have been a precedent, surely *unprecedented* is carelessly used here. The coverage (on all networks and in the press), however, produced an unprecedented amount of weird and wonderful verbiage: such words as *sortieing, weaponeering, interdiction* (in a sense other than the common one), *attriting, aggressing,* and dozens more. Quite a few such terms that I'd never heard before, let alone ever thought of using, turned out to have dictionary support. Others didn't. One of the most amusing sidebars came in reference to the processing plants that Gulf countries rely on to convert sea water to fresh water. The people talking about them were never quite sure whether to use *desalination* or *desalinization.* I watched an hilarious program in which the Westerners were using both words, sometimes stumbling badly when they started to say one and tried to switch to the other in mid-word. There was an urbane Saudi official in the conversation, and he referred to the process as *desalting*, which, of course, is precisely the correct word. The others didn't pick up on this at all. Probably they considered it an inelegant word.

A news story about a little-known Canadian actress stepping into a role at the Stratford festival said that "she is familiar to the stage". That smacks of anthropomorphism. I think it might have been more relevant to let us know if the stage is familiar to her.

Why are so many saying and writing "momento" instead of *memento*? Is a momento a reminder of a momorable mement, perhaps?

I can't think of anything much more trivial to gripe about than this line from a CNN anchorman who had just read a bulletin: "We will have more details as they become available." I think he meant *when*, not *as*, but, even at that, the point is that it is a remarkably fatuous statement. He might have said that they would update the report immediately upon receiving more details, or he might have suggested that we stay tuned for further details, if he had to say anything at all. He didn't really have to. It's just one of those things they do.

One of the side-effects of Western interest in the Gorbachev years in Russia was the way in which it forced us to re-examine English terms that we had come to take for granted without thinking much about their actual meaning. The problem was presaged by an anecdote (probably apocryphal) dating from a visit by Nikita Khrushchev to the United States. The story was that Mr. K. was being shown around a major U.S. factory by its owner, and was inquiring about working hours. He was amazed when told of the thirty-five-hour week and the coffee breaks and overtime pay and the rest of it, and said that in the Soviet Union, workers put in sixty hours a week and were not pampered in these other ways. To this, his capitalist host replied "We could never get away with that here — these union guys are a bunch of commies".

For decades, the West in many ways associated *communism* with the government of the U.S.S.R., casually overlooking the fact that the essential reality of that government was totalitarianism first and communism second. Communists were anti-capitalistic and un-American, and so on. They were extreme left-wingers and radicals. Anti-communists were right-wingers and conservatives. With the coming of *glasnost* and *perestroika*, we in the West were forced to cope with the idea that in Russia, communists were right-wingers and conservatives, and reformers of a capitalistic bent were left-wingers and radicals. It was a bit like watching a hockey game in a mirror. The reversals of left and right, of liberal and conservative, of radical and reactionary, required a fair amount of mental acrobatics, but it was a useful exercise. We all should more frequently take a fresh look at the words and phrases we use so readily.

"Almost every section of the city", Lloyd Robertson told us in a CTV newscast, "has sustained serious damage." If he meant that almost every section had borne up under serious damage without being destroyed, we have no quarrel with him. I suspect, however, that he meant *suffered*. If so, he should have said that, or simply said "was seriously damaged". *Sustain* sustains more serious damage at the hands of modern journalists who keep telling us that "the accident victim sustained a broken leg", a barbarism now condoned by too many dictionaries. The word is most useful in its sense of maintain or keep going. Its extension (which dates from the fifteenth century) to mean endure is useful, but there is no reason to use it as a substitute for *suffer* or *receive*. As Fowler says, "if it is not made to do the work of those more suitable words, it calls up more clearly the other meaning in which it is valuable". That's a piece of advice worth framing.

Credible is another word that is taking a terrible kicking around these days. I've been wondering for weeks what *Time* magazine meant when it said Ronald Reagan "performed credibly" as governor of California. The man is a former actor. Was this a theatre review? *Credible* means a bit more than believable; it implies trustworthiness. It sometimes gets into print as *creditable* (meaning praiseworthy), and vice versa. Could that be what happened? I would be prepared to believe anything of a magazine that (in the same issue) spoke of something being "razed to the ground", which is as bad as saying someone was killed to death.

A news service referred to "Iran's demands for the release of the hostages". Iran wasn't demanding the release of the hostages. The writer should have said "Iran's conditions".

An editor should have no compunction about disciplining the writer who told us that the Speaker of the House of Commons "is under no compunction to justify his decisions"; indeed, he should be under some compulsion to do so. The same writer probably would say "mitigated against" instead of "militated against" (and why not? — I've heard the acting prime minister say it), and the fact that this is a common malapropism should not mitigate the punishment. (Oddly enough, I've never heard anyone use *mitigant* for *militant.*)

I have seen and heard many lawyers being either indifferent to, or ignorant of, the distinction between *flout* and *flaunt.* Of all professions, surely law is one in which precision of speech is essential, and a lawyer who flaunts such ignorance possibly might not be depended upon not to flout the law. Some lawyers, as noted earlier, also have trouble with *impugn* and *impute,* and some writers need to be reminded that *turgid* and *torpid* are not interchangeable, any more than are *perpetrate* and *perpetuate* or *enormity* and *enormousness* or *harangue* and *harass.*

There is no such word as "ancilliary". A person who benefits from something is the *beneficiary*, not the benefactor. One doesn't answer a *how* question with *because. The reason why* and *the reason is because* are (or should be) unspeakable.

A loathsome practice creeping into the entertainment pages of the newspapers is that of using *delight* in an ambiguous manner. It may be used as either a transitive or an intransitive verb to mean give great joy or pleasure. As an intransitive verb, it can also mean be highly pleased or rejoice. Consider this headline on a *Toronto Star* theatre review: "Dunsmore delights in As You Like It". The reader is left to wonder whether what follows is a report that the actress gave her audience much pleasure or a report that she likes the play very much. The intransitive use to mean give pleasure is a recent development that is unnecessary and invites confusion. The prudent writer will eschew it.

Should you check the etymology of *delight,* you might be as startled as I was to discover that it really should be spelled "delite". Its origins had nothing to do with light. About 500 years ago, it was so commonly misspelled as *delight* (to match the likes of *light* and *flight*) that the corruption came to be accepted as the correct spelling. This kind of thing has been going on for a long, long time, but I would like to point out that this particular transition took almost a century to become established, whereas today, with the aid of TV and permissive lexicographers, it would take about twenty minutes.

I have a letter from someone who collected a list of goofs committed by CBC "personalities" and just plain announcers. He says, for instance, that some of them are so upset by the fact that there is no such word as *destruct* that they are determined to coin it, as both a noun and a verb. Alas, it has long been used behind the scenes in journalistic circles, as in "Let's do a destruct on so-and-so". You will also see it used, by sloppy people, instead of *destroy.* Anyone who uses it in any way deserves to be destructed.

He also mentions "mischievious", which is a widespread vernacular corruption of *mischievous.* It may not be a real word, but I like it. I just think it's more expressive with the extra syllable and the shift in emphasis, and it has a permanent place in my colloquial vocabulary. Dialect can contribute mightily to idiom. But I go along with his objection to such pleonasms as "halt and lame" and "clear and limpid". *Halt* means lame and *limpid* means clear, and it is limpid that no halt excuse for the use of either phrase is acceptable.

People love to quote Sam Goldwyn's famous "gaffe": "A verbal contract isn't worth the paper it's written on." It still gets laughs, but it isn't even a gaffe. Written contracts are verbal. Had he said "oral contract", that would be funny. *Verbal* doesn't mean unwritten. *Oral* does.

I have read and heard, from various sources, reports of people being killed while walking on the railroad tracks "while wearing portable headphones". I know what is meant, but it makes me wonder. How could one walk on the tracks wearing non-portable headphones, if there is such a thing?

Guerrilla evolved from meaning a small war to meaning one who is a soldier in an insurrection. What's done is done, but there may still be time to stop the now-spreading use of *guerrilla* as a synonym for terrorist.

It's difficult to get through a day without running into someone who doesn't know that *criteria* is the plural of *criterion*.

I'm certainly no expert, but I watch quite a bit of baseball on TV. I try to turn off the editor in my head, but don't have much success. I'm willing to allow sports writers and broadcasters a lot of leeway, as I've said elsewhere. I do want them to use colourful and innova-tive language. But the announcers and commentators, generally, are atrocious speakers, and when I hear one say that the pitcher "just beaned the hitter on the knee", I start climbing walls. Can't they even get a baseball term right? To bean someone is to hit him on the head. Period. Saying "beaned him on the knee" is akin to saying a wrestler has applied a chokehold to his opponent's ankle.

These people often use the term "shoestring catch", which is ridiculous. There are shoestring tackles in football when the tackler makes a headlong dive to catch the runner by the instep, but a div-ing catch has nothing to do with shoestrings.

I've never found a commentator who doesn't use *hitter* and *bat-ter* interchangeably. A batter is someone who tries, with or without success, to hit the ball. A hitter is a batter who hits the ball. You don't bean the hitter, you bean the batter. If he was the hitter, he wouldn't be standing at the plate waiting to be beaned, he would be running to first base. If he gets there safely and stands still, he is no longer the hitter, he is the runner. The only time you could bean a hitter is while he's still running to whatever base he stops on.

A CTV interviewer, talking to Canada's first female astronaut, asked her if the experience of looking homeward from orbit had given her "a less mundane view of our world". When you think about it, perhaps *mundane* was not the best possible word to use in that context.

One is either satiated or one is not. "Well-satiated" is a silly phrase.

A respected educator spoke, on TV, of "entrepreneurialship".

A network anchor bragged: "As CTV reported more than a month ago, the federal government came up with a package today...".

"We made some inroads to their demands." This from a labour leader who apparently meant concessions.

A report of an earthquake in Iran made reference to the dead and "wounded". I think it a bit sacrilegious to refer to people being wounded, rather than injured, by acts of God.

Shirley Solomon, to a guest on her CTV talk show: "You are one of only two women rabbis in all of Canada, and I guess that makes you very special and unique."

U.S. president George Bush was long known to be almost as adept at mangling the language as was his vice-president, Dan Quayle. Just one typical example: he said he didn't want to "tip his hat to the enemy". I wonder if he'd tip his hand to a lady.

You are not very likely to sit "glued to the television set". You might sit glued to your chair with your eyes or attention glued to the TV.

A member of the Metropolitan Toronto council objected to some of his fellows "globe-trotting around the world".

Newspapers have columns, and thus have columnists. Radio and TV stations do not have columns, so it's silly to refer to their commentators as columnists.

"Let me ask you a question", said a veejay on the MuchMusic TV channel. "I guess it's rhetorical, because I don't know the answer to it."

For as long as television has been around, I've been listening to descriptions of parades and military ceremonies by commentators who don't know the difference between a busby and a bearskin.

It is not proper to refer to someone who has served a full sentence in prison and been released as a "convict".

Talk-show hosts, who deal nightly with guests promoting their recordings, got into a flap when compact discs came on the market. They felt it was somehow wrong to call a CD an album, and there is some justification for that worry. But I would like someone to explain to me why these same people never worried about calling a single LP an album.

News writers, presumably in an effort to avoid repeating the various forms of *say*, get pretty careless sometimes. Just for a change of pace, they will say that so-and-so "claimed" or "maintains" that... These are loaded words that carry an implication of mistrust, and are too often used when such an implication is not warranted.

Elegant has too many meanings to be of much use, but I still use it because I think it's an elegant word.

A reviewer of software wrote this in a computer magazine: "It has a couple of unique features that I haven't seen in any other computer program."

Effectual and *effective* do not mean the same thing. Tell your MP.

Toward the end of the 1980s, we readily adopted *perestroika* and *glasnost* into our language. Heard either of them lately?

Suddenly (or so it seems to me), hundreds of our professional communicators, particularly those using television, have decided that *plus* is a conjunction ("The victim was robbed of $40, plus he was severely beaten"). *Plus* does not mean and. It came into English as a mathematical term. It is the verbal expression of "+". It means in addition to, and can be so used in non-technical language. It has other acceptable uses as an adjective and noun, but to use it as a conjunction is a barbarism. Plus it makes you sound stupid. As I said in Chapter 3, ad writers love it for their own devious reasons, but they should not be imitated by responsible writers.

A report on the funeral of a Toronto businesswoman said "Family members came from Scotland to attend, as did her co-workers from her company".

"He nodded his head 'no'." And shook his head "yes"?

Listening to interviews with foreign entertainment celebrities, one gets the idea that the very first English phrase they pick up is "You know".

"Never has an issue been more demagogued than...".

For some reason, some TV programs have sportscasters doubling as weathermen, which might account for one of them saying that a weather system had not moved on to the east "as scheduled".

Is someone who is *appealing* to the Supreme Court more likely to win than someone who is not?

Some people who should know better went on and on during a CBC network radio discussion program, confusing perquisites with prerequisites.

The term is *heart-rending*, not "heart-rendering". Tell Teddy Kennedy, among others.

Astrology is not a science.

Revenue minister Otto Jelinek, the guy whose hand is always in your pocket, told Parliament that "the decrease in cross-border shopping will continue to escalate". *Escalate,* which is a back-formation from *escalator*, means increase or be increased gradually, so Jelinek (who was once a pretty good skater) was telling us that a decrease was going to increase. I've always wondered what all that spinning on ice did to a person's head.

A promotion for a program on The Learning Channel said that "inventions of the future are changing our lives today". I'm still trying to figure that one out.

One of the great bits of unconscious irony was delivered by a TV newscaster who informed us that, in Belfast, "two more hunger strikers are fighting for their lives".

One of my software manuals says "For additional questions please contact the manufacturer". Hell, I don't need any additional questions. What I want is more answers.

Bibliography

A Dictionary of Modern English Usage, by W. H. Fowler, second
  edition, revised by Sir Ernest Gowers, Oxford University
  Press, 1972
A Grammar of Contemporary English, by Randolph Quirk, Sidney
  Greenbaum, Geoffrey Leech, and Jan Svartik, Longman, 1972
American Tongue in Cheek, by Jim Quinn, Penguin, 1982
On Language, by William Safire, Times Books, 1980
Paradigms Lost, by John Simon, Penguin, 1981
Room's Dictionary of Confusibles, by Adrian Room, Routledge &
  Kegan Paul, 1979
The Canadian Style, by The Department of the Secretary of State,
  Dundurn Press Ltd., 1985
The Careful Writer, by Theodore Bernstein, Atheneum, 1977
The Elements of Style, by William Strunk Jr. and E. B. White, third
  edition, Macmillan, 1979
The Writer's Art, by James Kilpatrick, Andrews, McMeel &
  Parker, 1984
Wordstruck, by Robert MacNeil, Viking, 1989